Hedging Interest-Rate Exposures

HEDGING INTEREST-RATE EXPOSURES

Brian Coyle

FINANCIAL
WORLD
Publishing
THE CHARTERED INSTITUTE OF BANKERS

Financial World Publishing
IFS House
4-9 Burgate Lane
Canterbury
Kent
CT1 2XJ
United Kingdom

Telephone: 01227 818687

Financial World Publishing publications are published by
The Chartered Institute of Bankers, a non-profit making registered educational charity.

Typeset by Kevin O'Connor
Printed in Italy

ISBN 0-85297-445-0

Contents

Introduction

Risk and Interest-Rate Volatility

Interest-rate risk is the risk to the costs and therefore profits of a business from an adverse movement in interest rates. Every company that borrows funds or invests in interest-bearing financial instruments has some exposure to interest-rate risk. The risk arises from the volatility of interest rates in the financial markets.

Potentially, interest-rate risk is greatest for organizations with large amounts of interest-related assets or liabilities, particularly banks.

Why Are Interest Rates Volatile?

The general level of interest rates in a free market economy is determined largely by market forces (supply and demand for funds) although government influence or intervention also occurs, especially for short-term rates in the money markets.

Interest rates can shift substantially over a fairly short period of time. This has been a feature of financial markets since many were deregulated during the 1980s. Governments no longer *control* domestic interest rates, and following the globalization of financial markets, demand and supply of loans and investments can switch rapidly from one currency to another, causing large interest-rate changes.

Although governments no longer control interest rates directly, they still exert a strong *influence* on them through their economic policy objectives. The monetary authorities of the world's major currencies can prompt a rise or fall in the general level of interest rates by raising or lowering a key short-term interest rate as a means of controlling the rate of inflation and economic growth. This is a responsibility, for example, of the Federal Reserve in the US, the European Central Bank in the euro-zone countries and the Monetary Policy Committee of the Bank of England in the UK.

Longer-term interest rates are affected by the size of the government's borrowing requirement. To borrow in large amounts over a long term, a government normally will have to offer high interest rates in order to attract investors. This will in turn have a knock-on effect, raising interest rates on bonds and other longer-term debts.

How Volatile are Interest Rates?

Interest-rate risk occurs because of uncertainty about *future* changes in interest rates. The direction and extent of future changes cannot be predicted with reliability or accuracy. However the volatility of interest rates in the past could be a useful indicator of what might occur in the months or years ahead, and so of the potential scale of the risk for borrowers, lenders and investors.

The general level of interest rates is affected by the rate of inflation, and during periods of high inflation in the past, interest rates also have been very high. However, even when the rate of inflation is low, interest rates tend to rise or fall as the economy goes through an economic cycle, rates rising when the economy has been expanding and falling when the economy is about to enter, or has entered, a downturn.

Other Factors Influencing Interest-Rate Risk

Interest-rate risk depends on three factors:

- the volatility of interest rates
- the size of an organization's exposure to an adverse change in rates, and
- the duration of the exposure.

The *size of the exposure* is the amount of funds borrowed, or the amount invested, or available for investment, in interest-bearing instruments. A company borrowing $100 million for example, has an exposure one hundred times greater than a similarly sized company that has borrowed just $1 million.

The *duration of an exposure* affects risk because interest cost or revenue accrues over time. For a company borrowing $10 million at a floating rate of interest, an increase of 1% in interest rates will cost $200,000 extra if the loan has two years remaining to maturity (1% x $10 million x 2 years), but only $100,000 extra if the loan will mature in just one year's time.

The volatility of interest rates and the size and duration of an exposure combine to create an interest-rate risk.

Example 1
Alpha has borrowed $100 million at floating-rate interest. The loan has just over two years to maturity, and interest rates are reset every six months to 200 basis points (2% per annum) above the current six-month dollar LIBOR rate. Six-month LIBOR was 5.0% at the previous reset date, but has now risen to 6.5%.

Analysis
Alpha was at risk to an increase in the interest rate when LIBOR stood at 5.0%, a risk that subsequently materialized. The rise in LIBOR from 5% to 6.5% in six months is relatively large. If the rate were to stay at 6.5%

until maturity of the loan, the extra interest cost to Alpha from the increase would be about $300,000 (1.5% x $10 million x 2 years) over the two-year period. Alpha is still at risk to a further increase in LIBOR above 6.5%, but would benefit if the rate were to fall.

Example 2
Beta has borrowed $50 million by issuing five-year bonds at a fixed rate of 6% per annum. It could have borrowed instead at a floating rate of three-month LIBOR plus 100 basis points (1%). Soon after the bond issue, three-month LIBOR fell from 6.75% to 4%.

Analysis
If it could be assumed that three-month LIBOR will remain at 4% for the next five years, Beta will be paying more interest by borrowing at a fixed rate of 6% than by borrowing at a floating rate of 5% (4% + 100 basis points). The extra cost in interest over the five-year period would be $2.5 million (1% x $50 million x 5 years).

Summary

Swings in interest rates can have a big impact on profitability. Companies with significant exposures to interest-rate risk should adapt their approach to risk management. When the risk is high, management should adopt measures to reduce it. A decision to do nothing about exposures should be carefully considered, and should not be taken out of neglect or lack or awareness. Interest-rate exposures can be reduced and controlled (hedged), and this book describes the various hedging methods that can be used.

To understand hedging, in particular the purpose of each hedging method, it is important to appreciate the different aspects of interest-rate risk. These are explained briefly in the next chapter.

2

Interest-Rate Risk

Exposures to interest-rate risk are larger and more varied for financial institutions, particularly banks, than for non-bank (trading) companies. For non-bank companies, exposures arise from the risk of:

- a rise or fall in the general level of interest rates
- a change in the yield curve, or
- a rise or fall in interest rates in one currency (for borrowing or investment) relative to another currency.

The General Level of Interest Rates

A company's exposure to a rise or fall in interest rates depends on whether it has borrowed or invested at a fixed or a floating rate of interest, and for how long. For a borrower, there is a risk of higher interest charges by borrowing at a variable rate when a fixed-rate loan would have been cheaper, or by borrowing at a fixed rate when a variable-rate loan would have been cheaper. A similar (but opposite) risk faces the lender or investor.

For example, borrowing at a fixed rate of 6% per annum would be cheaper than borrowing at a variable rate of 6% initially, if interest rates were to rise over the loan period. On the other hand, borrowing at a fixed rate would be more expensive if interest rates were to fall.

The risk varies according to the likely direction of interest-rate movements in the future. When interest rates are thought to be at a peak and likely to fall, variable-rate borrowing would be less risky than fixed-rate borrowing. If interest rates are thought to be at the bottom of a cycle, companies might seek to borrow long-term at a fixed rate, to take advantage of low-cost borrowing before rates start to rise.

The problem of fixed versus floating-rate interest exposure is summarized in the diagram below.

Fixed Versus Floating-Rate Borrowing

Borrow at fixed rate	Borrow at variable rate

The risk That interest rates will fall	*Potential benefit* That interest rates will rise	*The risk* That interest rates will rise	*Potential benefit* That interest rates will fall

Low risk If interest rates are thought to be near the bottom of a cycle	*Low risk* If interest rates are thought to be near the top of a cycle

The risk is two-way and some risk is unavoidable for every borrower. The fixed-rate borrower risks a fall in interest rates and the variable-rate borrower risks a rise in rates. On the other hand, the fixed-rate borrower benefits if interest rates go up and the variable-rate borrower benefits from a fall in rates. The task for management in a company that borrows is how to minimize the downside risks. It could, for example, have a mix of fixed-rate and variable-rate loans, so that the adverse effect of an interest-rate change on some loans is offset by the benefits from the same change on other loans.

Timing of a Loan
A company wishing to borrow could try to minimize the interest-rate risk by anticipating a future change in interest rates and timing its loan accordingly. For example, a company might wish to borrow $10 million

for three years at a fixed rate, but expects interest rates to fall in the next few months. Instead of borrowing at a fixed rate now, it could borrow short term, perhaps on credit at a variable rate, and switch to a long-term fixed-rate loan after interest rates have fallen.

Example
A company anticipates a requirement in six months' time to borrow $100 million for five years. It would like to borrow the funds at a fixed rate of interest. Interest rates are low, and a fixed rate of 5% per annum could be obtained now on a five-year bond issue. Interest on a six-month deposit of $100 million would yield 4.5% per annum.

Analysis
Although the company does not need the funds for six months, it could decide to borrow now at 5%, and invest the money for six months at 4.50% until it is needed. In this six-month period, there would be a loss of 50 basis points (0.50%) per annum on the borrowing and reinvesting that would cost the company about $250,000 (0.50% x $100 million x 6/12). However, when the funds are needed, the cost of fixed-rate borrowing might have gone up to 6% for example. By borrowing earlier at 5% fixed, the company would have reduced its interest costs by $1 million per annum.

Choosing whether to borrow at a fixed or variable rate, and when to borrow, are important elements in financial risk management. Large companies in particular should plan their funding requirements over the long term, and borrow at a fixed rate when interest rates seem low. An ability to manage the mix of fixed rate and floating rate, switching from fixed to floating-rate funds or vice versa can help companies minimize their exposures to potential or anticipated interest-rate changes.

Risk for the Lender
The risk for the lender from an adverse movement in interest rates should be the mirror image of the risk for the borrower. Banks should prefer to lend at a fixed rate when interest rates are expected to fall and at a variable rate when interest rates are expected to rise. However, most long-term lending by banks is at a variable rate. Because most of their

funds from customer deposits and interbank loans, are either short-term or obtained at a variable rate, a bank is largely protected from adverse movements in the general level of interest rates. If interest rates go up or down, banks still should be able to make a profit from the spread between:

- their variable rates receivable on loans to customers and
- the variable rates payable on deposits placed with them, or the cost of their short-term funding.

Risk for the Investor
An investor in marketable interest-bearing instruments is at risk from changes in interest rates and a consequent fall in the market value of his investment. When interest rates go up, the market value of existing fixed-rate investments will fall.

Example
The market value of 4.25% Treasury stock, redeemable in 30 years' time, is 98.60 ($98.60 per $100 face value of the stock), giving investors a current interest yield of around 4.3% per annum (approximately 4.25% x 100/98.60).

If interest rates were to rise, and investors expected an interest yield of 5% on this stock, its market value would fall to about 85 (4.25%/5% x 100). An investor holding $1 million (nominal value) of the stock would see a fall in the market value of the investment from 98.60 to about 85.00, causing a loss of over $100,000 ($986,000 – $850,000).

Yield Curve

A yield curve describes the relative fixed rates of interest on loans or investments with differing terms to maturity. In the US, a yield curve can be constructed from rates for Treasury bills, notes and bonds. In the UK, a yield curve for borrowing rates up to a term of one year can be constructed from yields on government securities.

Example 1

US Treasury bills, notes and bond rates are as follows:

Term	Rate %
One month	3.0
Two months	3.7
Three months	3.8
Six months	3.9
One year	4.2
Two years	5.3
Three years	5.8
Five years	6.7
Seven years	7.0
Ten years	7.4

The yield curve on the page opposite can be constructed from these figures. In this example, the yield curve slopes upwards, this means that interest rates are higher for bills and bonds with a long term to maturity. This is the normal yield-curve slope.

Upward Sloping (Normal or Positive) Yield Curve

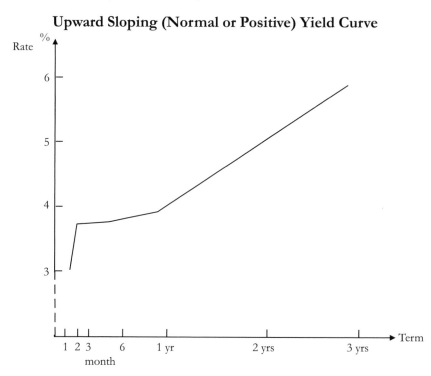

Although the yield curve uses Treasuries rates, these benchmark rates will be indicative of current yields for other instruments and loans of differing maturities in the rest of the US financial markets. For example, when the yield curve for Treasury bills slopes upwards, we should expect a one-year term loan to carry a higher rate of interest than a three-month loan.

Example 2
Yield curves can at times be downward-sloping or inverse. The hypothetical sterling LIBOR rates in the table below and illustrated in the graph are for an inverse yield curve, where interest rates are higher for short maturities.

Term	LIBOR rate %
Overnight	8.000
One week	7.125
One month	6.000
Three months	5.875
Six months	5.750
One year	5.625

Inverse Yield Curve

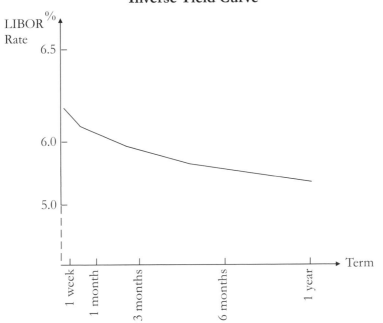

13

An inverse yield will exist when the markets anticipate a fall in interest rates at some time in the foreseeable future. For example, a bank might be willing to lend at a fixed rate for two years at 5.5% per annum, even though three-month LIBOR is higher, at 6% for example, if it expects short-term rates to fall below 5.5% in the near future.

Risk and the Yield Curve

The interest-rate risk associated with the yield curve is that the slope of the curve might change at some time in the future, from positive to negative or vice versa. For a borrower, this could mean that the choice of the term of borrowing, or the choice of time period between rollover dates on a floating-rate loan, could prove to be more expensive than an alternative borrowing term. Similarly, for an investor the risk is that a change in the slope of a yield curve could make the choice of maturities for investments less profitable than other alternatives.

Example 1

A company wishing to borrow $20 million for three years arranged a floating-rate loan with its bank. The bank offered a choice between interest at six-month LIBOR plus 100 basis points (1%) with six-monthly reset dates, or interest at one-year LIBOR plus 100 basis points, with annual reset dates. The interest rates were 5.875% for six-month LIBOR and 6.0% for one-year LIBOR. The company opted for six-monthly reset dates.

Over the period of the loan, interest rates were as follows:

After	Six-month LIBOR %	One-year LIBOR %
6 months	6.000	–
1 year	6.125	6.000
1½ years	6.125	–
2 years	6.250	6.125
2½ years	6.250	–

Analysis

By the end of the first year, there has been a change in the slope of the yield curve. Originally, the yield curve sloped upwards between maturities of six months and one year, LIBOR was at 5.875% for six-month borrowing and 6% for 12-month borrowing. After one year, and also after two years, the one-year rate was lower than six-month LIBOR, and the yield curve was inverse.

In retrospect, it would have been cheaper to opt for one-year rollover periods.

Interest payable at LIBOR plus 100 basis points

Year	Six-monthly reset dates %	Annual reset dates %
1	6 months at 6.875%	7.000
	6 months at 7.000%	
2	Full year at 7.125%	7.000
3	Full year at 7.250%	7.125

The interest cost in total over the three-year period would have been about $37,500 less if annual rollover dates had been selected.

A further risk with the selection of the borrowing or investment term is that the general level of interest rates could rise or fall adversely in the period to maturity of the loan or investment.

Example 2
A company borrowed $10 million for one year at LIBOR plus 200 basis points when one-year LIBOR was 7.5% and three-month LIBOR was 7.75%. Soon after the loan was transacted, interest rates fell. One-year LIBOR fell to 5.625% and three-month LIBOR to 5.5%.

Analysis
In this example, the yield curve has changed from inverse to positive, but more significantly, the general level of interest rates has fallen by approximately 2%.

In retrospect, the company made the wrong choice by borrowing for one year at a fixed rate of 9.5%. By choosing a variable rate loan with three-monthly rollover dates its costs on a $10 million loan would have been as follows:

	Interest rate %	Interest cost (approx) $
First three months	9.75	243,750
Months 4-6	7.50	187,500
Months 7-9	7.50	187,500
Months 10-12	7.50	187,500
Total interest cost with three-monthly rollover dates		806,250
Cost of one-year loan at 9.5%		950,000
Extra cost of 12-month borrowing		143,750

Basis Risk and Gap Exposure

Banks and other financial institutions are likely to have gap exposures and exposures to basis risk.

Basis risk occurs when a company raises funds on one interest-rate basis, and relends or invests on a different basis. For example, a bank might borrow regularly from customers at 1% below the three-month LIBOR rate and invest the funds in 91-day (three-month) Treasury bills. If three-month LIBOR is 7% and Treasury bills yield 6.5%, the bank would make a profit of 0.5% (6.5% - 6%) on its activities. Basis risk would exist, however, because interest rates on LIBOR and Treasury bills do not rise or fall in step with each other at all times. The interest rate on one basis, e.g. LIBOR, could go up or down by more than the interest rate on a different basis, e.g. Treasury bills. Continuing the same example, if three-month LIBOR went up by 1% to 8%, and the Treasury bill rate went up by just three quarters of 1% to 7.25%, the bank would borrow at 7% and invest at 7.25%, giving it a profit margin now reduced to just 0.25%

Gap exposure occurs when borrowing and relending is on the same basis, such as LIBOR, but there is a time gap between the reset dates for borrowing and lending.

Example

A bank borrows at three-month LIBOR and relends the funds three days later at three-month LIBOR plus 0.50%. There is no basis risk because both borrowing and relending are related to LIBOR. However, a gap exposure exists because the interest rate on borrowing is reset every quarter three days earlier than the interest rate on the lending. There is the risk of an adverse movement in interest rates in the three-day gap between the two dates.

Measuring Losses

Exposures to interest-rate risk result in losses when interest rates move adversely, and the exposures have not been hedged. Losses can be expressed either:

- as an opportunity cost, or
- as a fall in the value of a financial asset, or an increase in the value of a financial liability.

Opportunity Costs

An opportunity cost is the benefit forgone by choosing one course of an action instead of an alternative. For example, suppose that a company decides to borrow for five years at a variable rate of LIBOR plus 100 basis points, instead of at a fixed rate of 7% per annum, and at the time of making this decision, LIBOR was 6%.

The company is exposed to a rise in LIBOR over the five-year term of the loan. If LIBOR were to go up by 50 basis points to 6.5% for example, the borrowing cost would also rise, to7.5%. Compared with the option of borrowing at a fixed rate of 7%, borrowing at a variable rate would now be more expensive, by 50 basis points per annum.

If the size of the loan were $1 million, the opportunity cost of borrowing at a floating rate rather than a fixed rate could be expressed as approximately 0.50% x $1,000,000 = $5,000 per annum.

Marking to Market

Another way of looking at the cost of an adverse movement in interest rates is to measure its effect on the value of the organization's interest-related assets or liabilities. Market valuations can be obtained or estimated, using pricing models, for all types of financial instrument. Marking to market is the process of:

● revaluing assets or liabilities to a current value
● comparing the new value with a previously measured value
● recording the rise or fall in value since the previous valuation as a financial profit or loss.

Suppose for example that a bank holds $100 million (nominal value) of fixed-interest bonds. Due to a rise in interest rates, the market price of the bonds falls from 102.0 to 100.5. The loss to the bank is $1.5 million.

	$ million
Previous value	102.00
Current value	100.50
Loss incurred	1.50

Summary

Interest-rate risk occurs from choices about how, when and for what term to borrow, lend or invest. The risks are likely to be greatest for companies and institutions that borrow, lend or invest heavily, notably banks, but many other companies have significant interest-rate risks.

Management should understand the interest-rate exposures their organizations face. Exposures should be monitored regularly, and a hedging policy should be in place to manage the risks.

3

Identifying Interest-Rate Exposures

To decide whether its interest-rate exposures are significant and whether a policy of exposure management should be introduced, a company should first identify what its exposures might be.

Assessing the Potential Size of Risk

All companies, even small ones, should be able to check the possible scale of their interest-rate risk. If there might be a possibility of a large exposure to risk, further analysis should be undertaken. If the potential risk seems low or non-existent, no further action need be taken unless circumstances change, for example when the company decides to seek a large new loan. There are three simple ways in which a non-bank company can assess the potential scale of its exposures:

- balance-sheet analysis
- profit-and-loss-account analysis
- industry analysis.

Balance-Sheet Analysis

The presence of a relatively high amount of debt in a company's balance sheet is a fairly reliable indicator of high interest-rate exposure. Financial gearing, or leverage, is the most widely used measure of the scale of balance-sheet debt. There are several ways of measuring gearing, all of them broadly similar. One typical definition is:

$$\text{Gearing} \quad = \quad \frac{\text{Finance debts}}{\text{Share capital} + \text{Reserves}} \quad \text{x} \quad 100\%$$

Although market valuations could be used for both debts and share capital, in which case the balance-sheet reserves would be excluded from the measurement, it is usual to take balance-sheet valuations for debt, share capital and reserves.

Finance debts consist of bank loans and overdrafts, commitments under hire purchase and finance lease obligations, bonds, debentures, loan stock, commercial paper and other borrowing instruments.

High gearing is an indication of high interest-rate exposures for the borrower and suggests a high credit risk for the company's lenders, with a significant risk of default should there be a fall in profits or an increase in interest rates. This need not be a problem if the loans are at a low (fixed) cost and long term or if the company has high profit margins that can support the debt burden.

However, in general, a quoted company's share price is likely to fall progressively as the gearing increases beyond what is perceived to be the optimal level. Deciding whether a company's gearing level is indicative of high exposure to interest-rate risk calls for some rule-of-thumb judgment. As a rough guide, if debts exceed share capital and reserves, and if the ratio exceeds 100%, the company's management should consider establishing a formal system for monitoring its exposures. However, perceptions of what is high gearing can vary according to circumstances in the financial markets. For example, higher gearing is less risky when interest rates are low.

Profit-and-Loss-Account Analysis

A useful guide to interest-rate exposure can be extracted from a company's profit and loss account. A company must be able to pays its interest costs out of its profits. The most widely used ratio for analysis is *interest cover*. This is simply a measure of how large the company's profits are in relation to its interest charges.

$$\text{Interest cover} \quad = \quad \frac{\text{Profit before interest and tax (PBIT)}}{\text{Interest costs}}$$

At the very minimum, PBIT must be high enough to pay interest and other financial charges. In practise, profits should be substantially higher than interest costs otherwise the company will be at serious risk of insolvency. Interest cover is low if it is less than 3.0 times, in other words if PBIT is less than three times as large as interest costs. It is dangerously low if it is less than 2.0 times because it would take a fairly small drop in the volume of sales or in profit margins to reduce profits to a level where they were insufficient to cover interest costs. Equally damaging for a company with low interest cover would be an increase in interest rates on floating-rate borrowings. As a general guide, a company with an interest cover below 3.0 times should consider a formal system for monitoring its interest-rate exposures.

Example
A company with profits before interest and tax of $3 million incurs interest charges of $1.5 million.

Analysis
The interest cover of 2.0 times (3.0 ÷ 1.5) is low, indicating a high-risk financial position. If the company is financed largely by variable-rate loans, it is helpful to remember that an increase of 1% in interest rates would cost an extra $10,000 per year for each $1 million borrowed at variable rate.

The company's management would be well-advised to monitor its interest-rate exposures and consider hedging them.

Industry Analysis
Some industries are more vulnerable than others to changes in interest rates, and companies in these industries should be aware of their interest-rate exposure. House building is a notable example: house-building companies have to finance development work with substantial borrowing. If interest rates rise, higher home-loan rates are likely to

depress the demand for houses. House builders will suffer from unsold houses and cash flow difficulties, as well as the risk of lower house prices and declining profit margins.

Other industries vulnerable to interest-rate changes include consumer appliances, motor car manufacture and sales, airlines, tour operators, property development and investment as well as any industry where the level of demand is linked to the rate of economic growth, such as financial services.

The following table summarizes guidelines for deciding whether to establish a system for measuring interest-rate exposures. If potentially a company is a high risk for gearing, interest cover or industry, a system for measuring exposures would be advisable.

	Nil risk	Low risk	Possible high risk
Gearing	Nil gearing	Gearing below about 50%	Gearing of 100% or more
Interest cover	No interest charges	Cover greater than 5.0 times	Cover of less than 3.0 times
Industry	-	-	Construction, property, and other industries relying on high levels of borrowing to operate and susceptible to changes in interest rates and the economy

Measuring Interest-Rate Exposures

If a company suspects that its interest-rate risk might be high, measured by the three broad indicators described above, it should identify and quantify the size of the exposures, and structure a *systematic* approach to identifying interest-rate exposures.

Three techniques that can be used are:

- building a profile of exposures
- cash flow forecasting
- gapping techniques.

Building a Profile of Exposures

One approach is to build up a profile of existing and anticipated exposures for borrowing or investments in each currency. For each currency, a company could establish:

- its total borrowing and investments and
- the interest basis for variable-rate items, e.g. borrowing at LIBOR plus 150 basis points, or the actual rate of fixed-rate borrowing, e.g. 7% fixed, and the amount borrowed in each case.

For each interest rate or interest basis of borrowing, loans could be sub-grouped by maturity (time periods).

Profiling exposures would show the sensitivity of the company's profits to interest-rate fluctuations in each currency in different time periods.

Example
A company might produce a profile of its sterling interest-rate exposures as follows:

Alpha Inc
Interest-rate exposures as at June 1 Year 1

	Fixed-rate loans			Variable-rate loans	Total loans
	Existing $ million	Anticipated $ million	Total $ million	$ million	$ million
Now	47	-	47	55	102
End Year 1	44	-	44	55	99
End Year 2	40	54	94	30	124
End Year 3	40	50	90	30	120
End Year 4	40	50	90	30	120
End Year 5	0	50	50	30	80

Maturity profile:
Fixed-rate borrowing
Existing loans

Maturing Year 1	$3 million six-month loan at 9%
Maturing Year 2	$4 million one-year loan at 7.5%
Maturing Year 5	$40 million ten-year bond at 6.25%

Variable-rate Borrowing

Maturing Year 2	$25 million at three-month LIBOR + 1.5%
Maturing Year 3	$15 million at three-month LIBOR + 1%
Maturing Year 4	$10 million at three-month LIBOR + 1.25%

Renew loan maturing in Year 3
Renew loan maturing in Year 4
Unused credit facility of $5 million at base rate plus 1.25%.

The advantage of a profile of borrowings and investments is simplicity, provided the schedule of actual and anticipated loans does not become too long. The profile sets out how much borrowing the company has and expects to have, an analysis of the mix between fixed and floating rate and, where possible, the basis or cost of borrowing.

It can be used to assess the exposure to a rise or fall in interest rates. In the schedule above, for example, the company has fixed-rate borrowings of $47 million and floating-rate borrowings of $55 million. If interest rates were to fall by 1%, the company would still have to pay an unchanged rate on its fixed-interest borrowings, and would not benefit from the lower market rate. However, it would benefit from a lower annual interest charge of $550,000 on its floating-rate loans. There would be a net gain by way of a reduction in interest costs of $80,000. However, by the end of Year 3 when its fixed-rate loans are expected to be $90 million compared with variable-rate loans of $30 million, there will be a much greater exposure to falling interest rates.

For example, if the company expected interest rates to fall over the next year of so, its existing fixed-rate borrowings might still be cheap, but it might wish to defer the Year 2 fixed-rate bond issue until after rates had fallen.

The information in a profile of interest exposures could be used:

- for decisions about changing the mix of fixed and floating-rate loans, if the company anticipates an interest-rate change, or considers that it is over-exposed to either fixed or floating-rates of interest
- for business planning. The company could assess the potential impact of interest-rate changes on its future profitability.

Cash Forecasts

Cash forecasting, both short term and medium term, is important in any system for quantifying interest-rate exposures. A trading company must try to quantify, for each currency in which it has income and expenditure:

- its future net cash flows from operations, receipts from asset sales and investments, and
- expenditures for acquisitions, fixed-asset purchases, dividends, taxation and so on.

The cash forecasts should be analyzed by time periods. The length selected for each time period will be a matter of judgment, depending on the size and nature of the company's cash flows. In the very short term, up to one month, daily or weekly time periods might be appropriate. For slightly longer periods, from one month to six months, weekly or monthly time periods might be appropriate. In the long term, six months to five years, time periods of a month, a quarter, a half year or annually might be selected.

Example
A simplified cash flow forecast for a company might be as follows:

	Week 1 $000	Week 2 $000	Week 3 $000	Week 4 $000	July $000	Aug $000	Sep $000	4th qtr $000
Opening cash	- 750	- 770	- 680	- 680	- 728	- 740	- 1,105	- 967
Sales receipts	+300	+ 350	+ 270	+ 400	+ 1,200	+ 300	+ 1,600	+ 4,600
Supplier payments	- 120	- 180	- 160	- 280	- 750	- 200	- 900	- 2,800
Salaries	- 60	- 60	- 60	- 60	- 240	- 240	- 240	- 720
Other expenses	- 140	- 20	- 20	- 20	- 200	- 200	- 200	- 600
Capital expenditure	-	-	- 30	-	- 30	- 30	- 30	- 90
Receipts from asset sales	-	-	-	-	-	-	-	-
Dividends/taxation	-	-	-	- 100	-	-	- 100	- 100
Other income	-	-	-	+ 20	+ 20	+ 20	+ 20	+ 60
	- 770	- 680	- 680	- 720	- 728	- 1,090	- 955	- 617
Interest	-	-	-	- 8	- 12	- 5	- 12	- 31
Closing cash position	- 770	- 680	- 680	- 728	- 740	- 1,095	- 967	- 648

Interest payable over six-month period = $68,000
Maximum borrowings $1,105,000

Forecasts cannot be 100% accurate. They might not be even 75% accurate when the cash flows of the business can be volatile and uncertain. Some items in a cash forecast will be more certain than others, and the measurement of cash expenditures and income should be *qualitative* as well as *quantitative*. For example, an estimate of net cash income during one week might be $10 million, but a quantitative analysis could be:

- net cash income to be at least $8 million
- 80% probability (high degree of certainty) that it will be at least $9 million
- 50% probability that it will be at least $10 million
- 25% probability that it could exceed $11 million.

27

A cash forecast will indicate:

- what a company's funding requirements are likely to be
- how much funding will be long term and how much will be temporary
- the length of short-term funding requirements
- the size and duration of any cash surplus.

This analysis is needed to establish funding requirements, but it also will provide a measure of interest-rate exposures arising from the size of the company's debts and its interest charges, given the expected level of interest rates. A cash forecast can distinguish between fixed-rate and variable-rate payments and receipts of interest, to support an assessment of the fixed/floating-rate exposures of the company.

Future changes in interest rates also are difficult to predict, both as to the size of any change and also its timing. Therefore, companies might seek out views from economists employed by stockbrokers or investment banks. Decisions about whether to hedge a risk, or how to hedge a risk will depend on the finance director's or treasurer's judgment about which way interest rates are likely to move, by how much and when.

Cash forecasting should not be an occasional exercise. It should be a dynamic process with continual review of the timing and the amount of various component parts of cash flow, making revisions whenever necessary.

Gapping Techniques

The aim of gapping techniques is to identify the exposure of a company to changes in interest rates during each time period.

If a company has more floating-rate borrowings than variable-rate financial assets, there is a *negative* gap. An increase in interest rates will reduce profits. Most companies, except financial institutions such as insurance companies and banks, are in this position.

If a company has more variable-rate financial assets than variable rate borrowings, there is a *positive* gap. An increase in interest rates will boost profits and a fall in rates will reduce profits. Banks usually are in this position. Cash-rich companies also might have a positive gap.

Gapping techniques include maturity gap modeling, duration analysis and simulation modeling.

Duration analysis and computer simulation modeling are used by financial companies such as banks to analyze their interest-rate risk. Duration is explained in the appendix to this book.

Maturity Gap Models

The aim of a maturity gap model is to identify the gap in any future time period between the expected cash receipts from interest-rate sensitive assets and the expected cash payments on interest-rate-sensitive liabilities.

The first step in constructing a maturity gap model is to decide what the gapping period should be, every quarter, month, week, day. A shorter gapping period gives greater accuracy in the analysis. However, a gap model with short gapping periods is more difficult to use because interest-rate risk should be hedged separately for each gapping period. Daily gapping periods, for example, would require skilful management and hedging decisions taken for each operating day.

Data for the model must be collected and interest-rate items identified and recorded. Interest-rate-sensitive items are assets or liabilities that could be affected by changes in interest rates during the gapping period. Such liabilities, for non-bank companies, include:

- variable-rate bank loans for which the interest rate will be reviewed during the gapping period
- bank loans maturing during the gapping period, for which replacement/renewal of the loans might be required.

29

Interest-rate-sensitive assets include variable-rate bank deposits and investments such as government bonds, certificates of deposit and commercial paper.

The interest income and interest payments for these assets and liabilities should be calculated or estimated for each gapping period. This is done by deducting interest outflows on interest-rate-sensitive liabilities from interest income from interest-rate-sensitive assets.

If the gap between the interest outflows and inflows is zero, there should be no, or very little, interest-rate risk during the gapping period. The greater the size of the gap, the higher the interest-rate risk will be. A negative gap of $1 million in net borrowings during a particular month, for example, would mean that the company is at risk to an increase in interest rates that could cost $100 per annum for each basis point (0.01%) increase.

4

Hedging Policy

Hedging means taking action to reduce or cover an exposure. It is the process by which financial risk is managed. The broad aim of hedging is to reduce the likelihood of poor profitability caused by adverse interest-rate changes. Hedging often has a cost, such as a fee payable to a financial institution or a potential reduction in profit margin, yet for most companies the costs can be justified by the reduction in risk.

The framework of an interest-rate exposure management system should be:

- to monitor and assess the organization's exposures
- to formulate policy aims and objectives for hedging exposures
- to select the suitable methods of hedging
- to review continually exposure management decisions, and make new decisions as appropriate.

Assessing Interest-Rate Exposures

Monitoring interest-rate exposures allows a company to assess the potential size and duration of the risk. There also should be a policy regarding what risks are acceptable, whether excessive risk should be avoided or existing risk reduced or contained.

Management should try to assess the seriousness of the risk from the company's measured exposures. There should be a continual assessment by a company of exposures to:

- the total amount of its borrowings or interest-yielding investments

- the balance of fixed and floating-rate loans or investments
- the term structure of loans or investments
- the maturity of existing loans and investments
- the currency of loans and investments.

Exposures, having been quantified, can be assessed simply by asking what if? For example, what if interest rates were to rise by 1% within the next three months? What if short-term rates were to fall by 2% and there is a change in the yield curve? What if the spread between LIBOR and certificate of deposit rates were to narrow by 15 basis points?

Management may have firm views about the probable direction and timing of future interest-rate changes that will influence their assessment of the risk. For example, if interest rates were expected to fall, a company with most of its borrowings at a floating rate of interest might consider its low proportion of fixed-rate borrowing beneficial rather than risky. On the other hand, if real rates of interest are expected to rise and remain high, a company might be concerned about its total borrowing exposure, especially over the longer term, and decide, if possible, to cut its borrowings by raising more equity finance.

Assessing the risk in the *term structure* of a company's loans and investments calls for judgment about the future shape of the yield curve (positive or inverse) and whether there might be a change from positive to inverse or vice versa. Suppose for example that the dollar yield curve is negative and that interest rates are higher for shorter-term than for longer-term instruments. A company with an interest-yielding dollar investment portfolio might have a large proportion of short-term investments, but take the view that the yield curve will become positive in six months to a year. Therefore it may decide that the interest-rate exposure from its sizable short-term investments is not serious at the moment, but that in several months, the situation could change, and a switch into longer-term investments could become desirable.

The maturity of existing loans also should be monitored. If a large number of loans mature at the same time, and the company expects to renew the loans to continue the funding of its operations, it will be exposed to an increase in the general level of interest rates before or around the time the existing loans mature.

The Need for Risk Management

Having assessed the seriousness of the risk, management will be in a position to decide whether to take action to reduce the risk, or at least prevent the situation from getting worse.

Financial risk management in non-bank companies has tended to concentrate on foreign exchange risk and credit risk, rather than on interest-rate risk. Losses from bad debts and foreign exchange losses are reported in a company's annual financial accounts. Losses from interest-rate changes, in contrast, are not reported because they are an opportunity cost. They occur because a borrowing or investment decision was made that in retrospect was not the most profitable or least-cost option.

However, interest-rate losses can be very high, particularly when interest rates are volatile and a company is funded largely by debt capital rather than by share capital and reserves. A change in the general level of interest rates by just 1%, for example, will reduce profits at the rate of $10,000 per annum for $1 million borrowed. In extreme cases, a company that is not generating enough cash income to meet additional interest costs could be forced into liquidation. More commonly, a company's bank loans or bond issues could have covenants that would be breached as a result of an increase in interest rates. A common loan covenant is that the interest cover ratio should not fall below a certain level. An increase in interest charges might cause a breach of the loan covenant for a company whose interest cover ratio was already close to the minimum acceptable, giving the lending bank the right to call in the loan if it wished.

Deciding whether to Hedge

The concerns of non-financial companies for managing interest-rate risk are likely to vary according to their reliance on debt capital funding. Financial companies, both banks and investing institutions, have continual interest-rate exposures. For banks in particular, these can be very substantial. If exposures to risk are fairly low, measures to limit or control them are perhaps unnecessary. When exposures to risk are high, however, there is a greater need for hedging action to reduce the risk. A basic approach to risk management is suggested on the next page.

An Approach to Managing Interest-Rate Risk

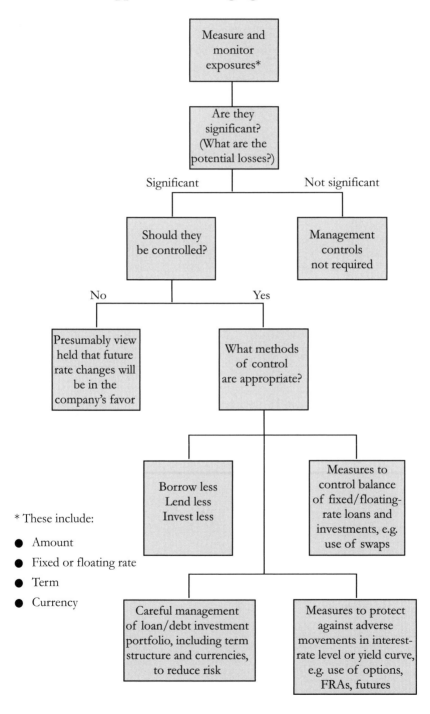

* These include:

● Amount
● Fixed or floating rate
● Term
● Currency

Formulating a Hedging Policy

A company with large interest-rate exposures should formulate a policy for managing them. Decisions about whether to hedge exposures should be taken periodically at board level, and more regularly at an operational level by the treasurer responsible for day-to-day exposure management.

The preferred policy could be one of not hedging any of the exposures, provided the company's management is aware of the risk and potential consequences of such an approach. More likely, the board will set down guidelines for hedging a stipulated proportion of the exposures. For example, hedging guidelines might be set for the company's exposure to floating-rate borrowings.

Companies with very large debt portfolios are particularly vulnerable to an increase in interest rates, so lending banks might wish to make it a *condition of lending* that the borrowing company take measures to hedge interest-rate exposures. More likely, however, a bank will impose loan covenants that stipulate a minimum interest cover level or maximum ratio for financial gearing.

Financial risk, remember, is normally a two-way risk, with an upside opportunity to benefit from favorable changes as well as a downside risk of losses from adverse changes. The reason for hedging an exposure to a financial risk is that either:

- the risk of an adverse change is greater than the risk of a favorable one, or
- an adverse change would have serious implications for the company's profitability.

Action to hedge interest-rate exposures will be taken only if:

- a company considers the risk to its profits from adverse interest-rate changes to be far more significant than the prospects of gains from favorable rate changes, or
- measures can be taken that reduce the risks without significantly affecting the prospect of gains from favorable rate changes.

Policy Aims and Objectives

Objectives of interest-rate exposure management are:

- to minimize net interest costs or to maximize net interest income.
- to contain the cost of borrowings below a target level.

Within these broad policy objectives, there can be a specific aim or several specific aims, as summarized below.

For borrowing	For investments/lending
To fix the cost of borrowing	To fix the interest yield
To secure a worst-case (maximum) cost of borrowing	To secure a worst-case (minimum) interest yield
To reduce costs, or reduce the risk of high costs, by switching from fixed to floating-rate interest payments, or vice versa	To improve yields, or reduce the risk of low yields, by switching from fixed to floating-rate investments, or vice versa
To match borrowing costs with investment yields, to reduce risk	To match investment yields with borrowing costs, to reduce risk

The Fixed and Floating-Rate Mix

A finance director or treasurer of any company that borrows large sums of money will have to take a view on the proportion of its debt that should be at fixed rate and variable rate respectively. Borrowing entirely at a fixed rate or entirely at a variable rate normally is imprudent when large amounts of borrowings are involved.

There could be company-specific circumstances that influence the choice between fixed and floating rates. For example, a company undertaking fixed price contracts, or contracts for which higher interest costs cannot be claimed back from the customer under cost variation clauses, might wish to lock in a certain rate and opt for fixed-rate funding. In contrast, a company in a highly competitive market might need greater flexibility to respond to changing market conditions, and so prefer variable rate funding that reflects current market costs.

For other companies, there can be lending covenants on bank loans that impose a minimum interest cost cover (ratio of profits before interest and tax to interest charges). In such cases the company might want to be certain of interest costs and opt for fixed rates.

To a considerable degree, the decision about the fixed/floating-rate debt mix will depend on the personal view of the finance director or treasurer about future changes in the general level of interest rates, or the shape of the yield curve.

Example 1

As an illustration, a fixed/floating-rate policy might be to:

- keep a minimum of 25% of debt at fixed rates
- keep a minimum of 25% of debt at floating rates
- vary the proportion of the remaining 50% of debt between fixed and floating, according to the current outlook for interest rates and current borrowing opportunities.

Example 2

Tango is a major engineering company with substantial debt. Its board of directors agrees a policy on the fixed and floating-rate mix. The policy is based on the broad view that in the middle of an interest-rate cycle when rates are rising but are expected to rise still further, or rates are falling and are expected to fall still further, the company should try to achieve a 50:50 mix of fixed-rate and floating-rate debt. As interest rates move through the cycle, and interest rates are nearing their expected peak or low point, the company will adjust the mix, introducing more fixed-rate or more floating-rate debt according to the direction in which rates are moving. However, the company will never reduce the proportion of either fixed-rate or floating-rate debt below a minimum of 30% of the debt mix.

Occasionally, a treasurer could spot what he or she considers to be a bargain opportunity in the yield curve for fixed-rate borrowing for a particular maturity. Outside bank lending, many of the markets for borrowing are window markets. An opportunity to borrow funds at a favorable rate doesn't happen often, and is unlikely to coincide with actual funding requirements. To seize the opportunity for cheaper funds, a company would have to be aware, through forward planning, of just how much funding it will need in the future and when. Then it can use opportunities in a window market, e.g. the eurobond market or commercial paper market, to pre-fund these requirements.

Interest-Rate Management and Debt Management

Interest-rate management must be consistent with debt-funding management, so that the debt portfolio matures in an orderly way. Companies with a large proportion of their debt maturing within a short time period could face serious problems with paying off their debts as they fall due, or with arranging re-finance.

It is important to appreciate that although there is a relationship between debt management and interest-rate management, the two activities can be separated. This is because after an initial decision has been taken to borrow funds (debt management) the cost of funds subsequently can be managed by purchasing derivative instruments, such as forward-rate agreements (FRAs), options or swaps.

Decisions on interest rates, once taken, can be adjusted by exposure management techniques through hedging action and without the need to arrange new loans or repay existing loans, provided a company regularly monitors its interest-rate exposures.

Speculating on Future Interest-Rate Changes

Often it will be very tempting for finance directors or corporate treasurers to make forecasts of future interest-rate changes, trying to identify the peaks and low points of the interest-rate cycle. By predicting when interest rates will go up, they might hope to arrange funding at the *lowest* possible interest cost.

For example, if a company wants to borrow $50 million for one year it might consider the following choices:

- to borrow for one year at today's fixed-interest rate for a one year loan
- to borrow for one year, but at a variable rate, with rates reviewed either after six months, (for the second six-month period of the loan) or after every three months.

The variable-rate option would be preferred if the company felt that the general level of interest rates were to fall soon or that the yield curve would change, with short-term rates falling relative to longer-term rates.

Example
A company borrowed $50 million one year ago at a fixed rate of interest, having chosen not to arrange a floating-rate loan with a six-monthly reset date or quarterly reset dates. The choice of a fixed rate was taken in the belief that interest rates would rise. Interest rates over the loan period were as follows:

	3-month LIBOR %	6-month LIBOR %	12-month LIBOR %
At the start of the loan	4.0	5.0	6.0
After three months	6.0		
After six months	7.5	8.0	
After nine months	8.0		

Analysis
If the company had borrowed at a fixed rate for one year, the interest cost would have been $3,000,000 ($50 million x 6.0%).

If the company had borrowed at a six-monthly floating rate the interest cost would have been:

	$
First six months	($50 million x 5.0% x 6/12)	1,250,000
Second six months	($50 million x 8.0% x 6/12)	2,000,000
Total interest cost		3,250,000

If the company had borrowed at a three-monthly floating rate, the interest cost would have been:

	$
First three-month period	($50 million x 4.0% x 3/12)	500,000
Second three-month period	($50 million x 6.0% x 3/12)	750,000
Third three-month period	($50 million x 7.5% x 3/12)	937,500
Fourth three-month period	($50 million x 8.0% x 3/12)	1,000,000
Total interest cost		3,187,500

In this case the cheapest option in retrospect would have been a 12-month loan, fixing the rate for the full period, and the company speculated correctly. However, it might have guessed incorrectly and opted for a higher-cost borrowing arrangement.

A danger with speculating on interest-rate changes by borrowing short term to finance *longer-term* funding requirements could be the difficulty of persuading banks to relend the required amount of funds when short-term loans mature, except at very high rates of interest. This is the so-called refinancing risk.

A risk-averse approach to interest-rate risk management, in contrast to speculative funding decisions, seeks to limit the risks of adverse interest-rate movements, but at the cost of losing the maximum benefit from any favorable interest-rate movements.

Company treasurers, in practise, often will try to mix the two approaches by:

- forecasting interest-rate changes and obtaining funds accordingly (speculative decisions) but
- seeking to hedge some of the risks in funding decisions whenever the cost of adverse interest-rate changes is seen to be high.

How Much to Hedge?

Deciding how much of an exposure to hedge calls for good judgment. Unlike foreign-currency exposures that can sometimes be 100% hedged, interest-rate exposures are almost unavoidable for a company with borrowings or interest-yielding investments. For example, if a company has an exposure to floating-rate borrowings and the risk of rising interest rates, it can switch into fixed-rate borrowing to hedge the risk. By doing so, however, it creates an exposure to the risk of falling interest rates.

Banks and other financial institutions must hedge their interest-rate exposures. The main business of a commercial bank is to re-lend money, and adverse changes in interest rates could be devastating unless exposures are hedged.

Broad Methods of Hedging Interest-Rate Exposures

There are two main approaches to hedging interest-rate exposures: structural hedging and market instruments (largely derivatives).

Structural hedging involves the balancing of amounts, currency and timing of interest-rate-sensitive cash flows in order to cancel out exposures. Methods of hedging with market instruments include both cash-market (money-market) products, such as deposits and loans, and also derivative products such as forward-rate agreements (FRAs), futures, swaps, options, caps, floors and collars.

In the chapters that follow, various hedging methods will be illustrated that for simplicity, use non-bank companies as examples. The same principles apply to hedging by banks, and it will be useful to bear in mind that the markets for some hedging instruments, such as interest-rate futures, are dominated by bank trading.

Summary

Companies should have a system in place for identifying their exposures. This will involve some forecasting of future funding needs and of the likely changes in interest rates. An interest-rate-exposure management system can be established in which

- exposures are identified
- objectives and strategies are set for exposure management
- action is taken where suitable to hedge exposures and
- all exposure management decisions are reviewed.

5

Structural Hedging

Structural hedging is a term that describes the reduction or elimination of exposures by controlling the structure of the company's balance sheet through careful management of cash flows, assets and liabilities. It can be applied to the management of both interest-rate exposures and foreign-currency exposures.

Structural hedging can be used to:

- match cash inflows and cash outflows as closely as possible so as to minimize the need to borrow. A feature of this type of hedging is the *netting* of cash flows
- match actual borrowed funds with the requirement for the funds, to avoid excessive borrowing or surplus funding
- match assets in one currency with liabilities in the same currency, to eliminate foreign currency exposures.

In the case of a bank, structural hedging will involve the matching of assets and liabilities (loans and deposits, etc.) for maturity or rollover dates, so that the bank's interest income and interest costs will rise or fall in tandem, to the extent that matching takes place, with any change in market interest rates. For example, if a bank regularly borrows a proportion of its funds at three-month LIBOR in the interbank market and relends those funds to corporate customers at LIBOR + 75 basis points with three-monthly rollover dates, there will be a matching of assets and liabilities. This will eliminate any interest-rate risk and secure a profit of 0.75% per annum before bad debts on the borrowed funds.

Netting Cash Flows

When a company has more than one bank account, there is a likelihood that idle cash balances will be held in some accounts when other accounts are in overdraft, or when the company has borrowed to cover cash deficits in other accounts. By matching cash inflows and cash outflows, a company's need for funds can be minimized.

Example
Alpha has three sterling bank accounts, but does not operate a system for netting surplus balances on one account against deficits on another. Its cash position in March Year 1 is as follows.

	Account 1 £000	Account 2 £000	Account 3 £000
Opening cash/(overdraft) balance	50	(40)	(10)
Cash inflows	25	35	50
Cash outflows	(40)	(25)	(65)
Closing cash/(overdraft) balance	35	(30)	(25)

At the end of the month, Alpha has surplus cash of £35,000 in Account 1 that it might transfer to an interest-yielding deposit. At the same time, it has overdrafts totalling £55,000 on Accounts 2 and 3, on which it is paying interest.

If Alpha had operated a policy of netting bank balances, its situation could have been as follows:

	Account 1 £000	Account 2 £000	Account 3 £000
Opening cash/(overdraft) balance	50	(40)	(10)
Transfers at start of month	(50)	40	10
Cash inflows	25	35	50
Cash outflows	(40)	(25)	(65)
Transfers during month	10	(10)	-
Closing cash/(overdraft) balance	(5)	0	(15)

At the month end, there is no surplus cash in any account, but the total overdraft is just £20,000. The interest-rate exposure therefore has been reduced to an exposure of £20,000 of variable-rate debt. In the non-netting situation the interest-rate exposure was £55,000 of variable-rate debt and perhaps £35,000 of variable-rate income.

In addition, net interest costs will be less with netting because the interest rate payable on loans will be considerably higher than the interest rate receivable on deposits. Hence structural hedging reduces both the exposure and the finance cost.

Companies often will have numerous bank accounts, in a variety of different currencies and in different countries. They will have to consider both currency risk and interest-rate risk in their structural hedging arrangements. Broadly speaking, if a foreign subsidiary has surplus cash in its bank account that is not needed to meet anticipated expenditures and the parent company has an overdraft, exposures can be reduced by transferring cash from the foreign subsidiary to the parent company and converting it into the parent's domestic currency. However, the *tax implications* of dividend payments from a subsidiary, or possibly even foreign-exchange control regulations, might also have to be considered.

Netting cash flows, although quite simple in theory, requires efficient management for proper control, and this might be one function of a centralized treasury department. A physical transfer of funds may not be necessary because a group of accounts at a single bank can be netted together without transferring cash between the accounts.

Overdraft Facility or Term Loan?

An overdraft facility can be negotiated that allows a company access to a nominated amount of funds. The company will pay for borrowed funds only when this facility is used, with interest charged daily on the amount overdrawn. In return for the facility, the bank will charge a front-end fee and a facility fee. An overdraft may not be a committed facility, in which case the bank is not obliged to provide funds on demand, and may refuse to do so in circumstances where it considers that the company's financial situation has deteriorated and lending more money would be too risky.

As an alternative funding measure, a company could obtain a term loan to finance its short-term cash requirement, removing the need for an overdraft. A term loan is drawn in full at the outset. The bank cannot withhold funds if the company's financial position deteriorates because the company will hold the full amount of the loan already.

Larger companies also have the option to borrow under a committed revolving credit facility that allows the company to borrow up to a pre-arranged limit on demand irrespective of the company's financial position provided it has not breached any set covenants under the loan agreement. In return for the flexibility of providing the certainty of extra funds on demand, a bank will charge a front-end arrangement fee and a commitment fee.

There is an interest-rate risk inherent in selecting one of these funding routes in preference to the others because the chosen route might prove to be more expensive. The relative cost of each method will depend on:

- the frequency with which the overdraft facility or committed facility will be used, this is uncertain and has to be estimated
- the size of the fee for each facility
- the returns obtainable on surplus funds, if the term loan option is chosen, although there will be some uncertainty as to the amount of surplus funds, the duration of the surplus and interest yields obtainable.

A term loan probably will be cheaper than an overdraft facility or a committed facility when the requirement for funds over the term of the loan closely matches the amount of the loan.

Matching Funding with the Need for Funds

At any time a company can have either more or less funds than it needs. When this happens, its interest-rate exposures will be larger than they should be, and structural hedging can reduce or eliminate the excess.

An interest-rate exposure can arise from a mismatch between the maturity of the borrowing and the maturity or end-of-useful-life of the assets that are being funded. Suppose that a company borrows to purchase an asset with a five-year life. If it obtains a five-year loan, the maturity of the loan and the asset will be matched. However, if it finances the asset with borrowing for a one-year term and renews the loan at the end of each year, the company will be at risk of an increase in the general level of interest rates, and also from a change in the yield curve, whereby one-year borrowing might become more expensive relative to five-year loans.

Suppose instead that a company raises a five-year loan to finance assets whose life is only one year. At the end of the year, there will be no assets, but a continuing debt obligation. The funds generated by the assets can be reinvested, but if interest rates have fallen, or if there has been a change in the yield curve, there will be a risk of the company having surplus funds whose interest costs exceed the investment-earning potential of the reinvested funds.

Example 1
A company wishes to borrow $5 million to invest in a fixed asset with a three-year life that would yield a total net cash return of $1,200,000. After deducting an annual interest cost of 6% or $600,000 ($900,000 in total over the three-year term), the project would earn a profit net of interest costs totalling $300,000 over the three-year period.

However, the company borrowed at a variable rate of interest, initially 6% with an annual rollover period, and interest rates changed over the term of the loan due to a shift in the yield curve and an increase in the general level of interest rates as follows:

	12-month rate
After one year	8%
After two years	9%

Analysis
The total cost of interest for the project will not be $900,000 (6% per annum for three years) but $1,150,000 (6% + 8% + 9% x $5 million).

This increase in interest costs would wipe out most of the anticipated profits from the project.

A risk-averse company should seek to match the term to maturity of its funding with expected life of the assets being financed. If circumstances change, for example by the acquisition of cash-generating business, the company's funding should be adjusted accordingly. By matching funding as closely as possible with the need for funds, a company will raise funds only when it needs to and for the required term. When the required funds are obtainable by borrowing, rather than by raising more equity capital, matching will involve:

- borrowing the amount of funds required, but no more
- borrowing at the time they are required, and not sooner
- borrowing for an appropriate *term*, to avoid the need for refinancing existing assets
- using an overdraft facility rather than term funding when the requirement for funds continually fluctuates with the trading operations of the company.

Example 2
Suppose that a company's forecast cash flows for six months are as shown.

A Six-Month Cash Flow Forecast

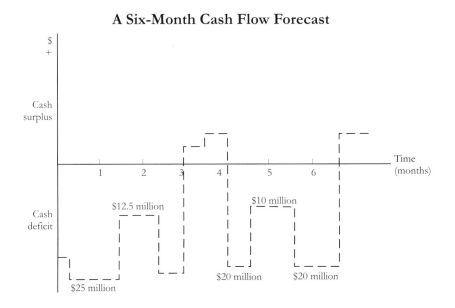

$25 million

Analysis

Some borrowing is required for most of the period to finance the cash deficit.

The maximum borrowing required is $25 million. However, a six-month loan of $250 million would be surplus to requirements for most of the period. An overdraft facility of $25 million also might be unnecessarily expensive.

A better matching of funding requirements could be a mixture of loans and an overdraft. For example:

● a three-month loan of $12.5 million for months 1-3
● a three-month loan of $10 million for months 4-6
● an overdraft facility of about $12.5 million or more, to allow for an unexpected shortfall in income or excess spending, for the full six-month period.

Long-Term Funds

Long-term funding requirements can be matched, ideally by long-term funds. For example, a capital project with an economic life of eight years could be financed by long-term borrowing of eight years, possibly at a fixed-rate of interest. Similarly, a need for continuous working capital of $50 million for one year could be financed by a one-year loan, at a fixed rate of interest for the full one-year period.

There are two problems with long-term funds, however. First, it is more difficult to borrow at a fixed rate for a long term, especially when interest rates are volatile and in circumstances where interest rates are rising or are expected to rise. Borrowings might have to be at a variable rate, and so there will be an exposure to rising interest rates. Secondly, borrowing at a fixed rate when interest rates are high will increase interest-rate exposure because the next movement in interest rates is more likely to be down than up.

Hedging in the Cash Markets

The cash markets are the markets for borrowing and lending, and include the bank loans market, the bond markets etc. A company can use the cash markets for structural hedging. It can try to match its portfolio of loans and investments to minimize or restrict interest-rate exposures, and to match its balance sheet assets and liabilities.

A company hoping to borrow should try to match the term of borrowing with the period during which the assets funded by the loan are expected to produce enough cash to repay the loan. A bank can borrow in the money markets to finance short-term loans to customers or other short-term investments. Money-market borrowing also is available to large companies wishing to fund their short-term requirements at the lowest possible cost. Companies with short-term cash surpluses can invest in instruments that mature when the surplus cash eventually will be required. In deciding on a fixed/floating-rate mix for borrowing, companies can try to obtain loans on the required interest-rate basis (fixed or floating-rate) in the loan or bond markets.

Arguments Against Structural Hedging

At some time or another, a number of companies, have deliberately built up a large amount of cash and money-market investments, and at the same time have borrowed large amounts of funds. This policy is the opposite of structural hedging that would use the cash surplus to pay off as much borrowing as possible.

There could be several reasons for borrowing when there is also surplus cash.

- *Convenience.* Long-term borrowing avoids the inconvenience of renegotiating loans as and when required, although it does create interest-rate exposures.
- *Contingency funding.* Some surplus funding might be required as a protection against the liquidity consequences of any potential business downturn.
- *War chest.* The management of an acquisitive company could accumulate cash in advance of a major acquisition.

- *Prefunding.* Identification of a future funding need can lead to premature funding in order to secure the cash before the funds are needed. There are several reasons for prefunding. An opportunity to raise money might be taken while funding is available from lending sources. If a company's credit rating is high, making borrowing easier, it could seize the opportunity to borrow in a particular market such as the eurobond market or the US Medium-Term Note market. And if interest rates were low, there could be an opportunity to borrow at a low cost before interest rates rose again.
- *Arbitrage opportunities.* Very large companies may be able to borrow funds in one market at one rate of interest and relend at a higher rate in another market so that the treasury department is acting as a profit center for the company. However, few companies are in a position to do this.

Summary

Structural hedging is the easiest and cheapest method of hedging interest-rate exposures, with judicious borrowing and lending in the cash markets. Many companies can operate safely with minimal interest-rate exposure by:

- maintaining positive net cash inflows from trading, with only occasional requirements for overdraft facilities, and
- keeping long-term debt requirements at a low level.

For companies with large borrowing requirements, however, structural hedging methods will reduce interest-rate exposures, but will not eliminate them. Debt invariably create exposures. These companies may then wish to hedge their exposures with treasury market products, such as swaps, futures, FRAs and options.

6

Hedging with Derivative Instruments

Various derivative instruments are available to hedge interest-rate exposures. These instruments derive from cash-market instruments, and have been created by banks and futures and options exchanges to form a separate but complementary financial market.

Forward/Forward Transactions

Prior to the advent of derivatives, an early technique of cash-market hedging was the forward/forward transaction. Although it is not much used today, it provides a useful starting point for an understanding of interest-rate management with derivative instruments.

The cash markets refer to lending and borrowing transactions and to cash transactions in the FX markets, because physical cash transfers of the principal amount are made. In contrast, in the derivative markets only interest flows are exchanged.

The purpose of a forward/forward transaction is to provide cover against the risk that interest rates will rise in the intervening time between now and when the borrowing will be made. It can be used to lock in an interest rate on a future loan or deposit.

A forward/forward transaction involves the combination of a cash market *loan* and a *deposit*.

- A company wishing to borrow a sum of money at a future date obtains a loan now at a fixed rate of interest.
- It deposits the borrowed funds now, for a shorter term, also at a fixed rate of interest, to mature at the start of the period from which the loan is required.

Example

In January, a company knows that it will want to borrow $10 million from the end of March until the end of September, and it wants to fix the cost of this borrowing now. It could do this with a forward/forward transaction by:

- borrowing $10 million now until the end of September, and simultaneously
- placing the $10 million on deposit until the end of March.

Analysis

The net cost of borrowing between the end of March and the end of September is fixed as the interest cost on the loan to September minus the interest receivable from putting the money on deposit until March.

Why are Forward/Forward Transactions Rarely Used?

Forward/forward transactions involve the simultaneous borrowing and depositing of funds that are not wanted. In the previous example, $10 million would be borrowed and deposited for three months, when the funds are not wanted by the borrower. Because there is no requirement for the funds, there is no reason why funds should be borrowed until they are needed. Borrowing and lending unwanted funds is cumbersome.

The same end-result could be achieved with less administrative effort and without the need to handle funds, by dealing in interest rates on notional funds, rather than physical loans and investments. Forward/forward transactions have been overtaken by a more sophisticated instrument, the Forward Rate Agreement (FRA), that is less cumbersome and a less expensive way of locking in interest rates on future short-term borrowings.

Why Use Derivative Instruments to Hedge?

Each derivative instrument explained in this book is used to hedge interest-rate risk in a particular way.

Instrument	Risk hedge
Forward rate agreement	An FRA can be used to fix an interest rate for a future loan or deposit starting within a period of one to 24 months. It also can be used to alter the interest-rate basis on a variable-rate loan to fixed rate.
Future	Short-term interest-rate futures (STIRs) are instruments that can be used to lock in an interest rate for a loan or deposit starting at a future date. They enable a company to protect itself against adverse interest-rate movements for up to 18 months or two years. STIRs are used primarily to hedge risk, but also can be used to speculate on future changes in interest rates. Speculators can make profits from correctly anticipating interest-rate changes. Bond futures can be used to lock in a value, and so a purchase or sale price, at a future date for a quantity of government bonds, thereby protecting bond investors against an adverse movement in the price of the bond in the intervening time.
Option	An interest-rate option gives its holder the right without the obligation, on or before a future date, to receive or pay a stipulated rate of interest for a specific period of time on a stated amount of principal. An option is a means of locking in a worst possible interest rate for either a loan or a deposit, and protects the option holder from adverse future movements in interest rates.
Swap	An interest-rate coupon swap enables interest-rate payments or receipts to be changed from a fixed rate to a floating rate, or vice versa, for a period of up to ten years or even longer. Swaps can be used to manage the mix of fixed-rate and floating-rate debt in an organization's funding structure without having to change the loans.

Derivative instruments serve two purposes for hedging interest-rate exposures. They can be used:

- to lock in a worst-case rate of interest for a period of time by setting a maximum fixed cost for borrowing, or a minimum fixed return on deposits
- to manage the fixed-rate/floating-rate mix in a company's debt or investment portfolio.

Swaps, FRAs, options and futures are not loans or deposits, and so are not cash-market instruments. By purchasing or selling derivative instruments a company with loans or deposits can manage the interest rates on them without having to change the underlying loans or deposits. Derivatives provide companies with greater flexibility in managing their interest costs.

For organizations with huge loans and deposits, banks in particular, derivative instruments can be valuable in reducing interest-rate risk. Banks are active in the derivative markets for two reasons:

- to make a profit or turn by acting as dealer or intermediary for clients, or
- to hedge their own interest-rate exposures that can be huge. This is why banks and inter-bank dealings still dominate the derivative markets.

Derivative instruments also can be used to speculate and make profits by taking a view on the likely future course of interest rates.

When to Buy or Sell?

One of the key decisions in any interest-rate hedging activity is choosing when to buy or sell. There are three elements that affect the decision.

- The amount of fixed-rate borrowing or investment, and when changes in these amounts occur.
- The amount of floating-rate borrowing or investment, and when changes in these amounts occur.
- Expectations about future interest-rate changes.

Which Instruments to Buy or Sell?

The choice of an appropriate derivative instrument for hedging will depend on the precise nature of the interest-rate exposure, although derivatives share similar risk reduction characteristics. For example, a company with a floating-rate loan seeking to hedge against an adverse change in interest rates for a period of up to 18 months to two years ahead could use a futures contract, an FRA or an option. The instrument chosen will either be the best or the most price-efficient hedge, or the most straightforward and convenient to use.

The instrument chosen should enable a company to achieve the purpose for which the hedge is being constructed, as set out in the following table:

	Interest rates expected to rise	**Interest rates expected to fall**
Fixed-rate borrower	Do nothing	Convert to floating-rate borrowing
Fixed-rate investor	Convert to floating-rate investment or sell the fixed-rate investments, if marketable	Do nothing
Floating-rate lender	Convert to fixed-rate borrowing or lock in a maximum interest rate for borrowing	Do nothing
Floating-rate investor	Do nothing	Convert to fixed-rate investment or lock in a minimum yield for the investments

The amount of the hedge should be a function of the size of the exposure, the proportion of the exposure the company wishes to hedge and management's judgment about future changes in interest rates, particularly the *direction* of future interest-rate movements, up or down.

Controls over Derivatives

Organizations buy and sell derivatives products for four main reasons:

trading
speculation
arbitrage
hedging exposures

mainly financial institutions

It can be difficult to make a clear distinction between these. A non-bank corporate, for example, might take a position with a derivative instrument as a hedge, but if the underlying transaction that is being hedged does not occur, the derivatives position will become speculative rather than a hedge.

A hedge can be defined as a transaction designed to produce a profit that largely will offset a potential loss from an exposure to financial risk. For example, if a company is set to suffer a loss of $10 million if interest rates were to rise by 1%, the hedge should be designed to create a counterbalancing profit of $10 million if interest rates were to go up by 1%. A hedge should relate to an exposure arising in the normal course of the organization's business activities. This definition of a hedge prompts several questions.

- How closely correlated must the hedging transaction be to the underlying business transaction? A hedge might not be perfect, so that the gain that would arise on the hedge might not exactly counterbalance any loss arising on the underlying business transaction.
- Should the hedge be kept in place for the full period of time that the exposure exists?
- Can a hedging position be closed when market prices such as the prices of futures create an opportunity for profit-taking, and reinstated later when market prices move the other way?

Controls over the use of derivatives should be applied to ensure that the organization's policy on hedging is properly applied, and that excessive risk (and speculation) is avoided. Key areas for control should be:

- Establishing a clear strategy, policies and procedures for entering derivatives transactions and for trading in derivatives
- A system of management supervision over derivatives activities, derivatives positions and exposures to risk
- A system for the accurate valuation of derivatives, with regular reporting based on marked-to-market values
- Procedures for measuring and controlling sensitivity, i.e. in identifying how movements in underlying variables, such as interest rates and exchange rates, will affect the value of the hedge
- Efficient execution and administration of derivatives transaction.

Valuation is a key element in the process of risk management with derivatives. Both the derivative instrument and the underlying instrument it is intended to hedge, if any, should be repriced regularly to their current market value (marked to market). In this way, the net gain or loss on positions can be monitored continually.

Few hedges are perfect. An organization should evaluate its derivatives as hedges in conjunction with the underlying position or instrument for which the derivative provides a hedge. The consequence for a hedge of any interest-rate movement or change in a currency exchange rate also should be understood.

The hedging functions of the main derivatives instruments will be considered in the following chapters.

Forward Rate Agreements (FRAs)

A forward rate agreement (FRA) is an over-the-counter (OTC) arrangement between a customer and a bank to fix an interest rate on a short-term loan or investment, starting from an agreed date at some time in the future. It is an agreement on an interest rate only and fixes a rate payable or receivable on a notional principal amount. It is not a contract to make an actual loan or investment.

For example, an FRA might fix the rate of interest at 6% on a notional three-month loan of $10 million, starting in two months' time. The parties to the FRA agree that the three-month rate of interest, three-month dollar LIBOR, for the loan will be 6%, regardless of how the market rate for three-month LIBOR moves in the next two months.

- To fix a *borrowing rate*, a company should *buy* an FRA from a bank specializing in such transactions.
- To fix an *investment yield*, a company should *sell* an FRA to the bank.

Because an FRA is independent of any actual loan or investment agreement, it cannot fix the rate for the loan or investment. Fixing the rate is achieved by means of a compensatory cash settlement between the parties to the FRA based on the difference between the agreed FRA rate and an index or benchmark rate of interest on or just before the settlement date. There is a payment from one party to the other that, taken together with the actual interest payable on the loan or receivable on the investment, produces a net amount payable or receivable, that is equivalent to the fixed FRA rate.

Example 1
Alpha expects to borrow $10 million for six months, starting in three

months' time on May 4, but is concerned that interest rates might go up before the loan period begins. Alpha will then borrow at six-month dollar LIBOR plus 100 basis points.

Alpha can buy an FRA from its bank that will fix the interest rate for six-month LIBOR at 6.5% per annum on a six-month loan of $10 million starting in three months' time on May 4.

Analysis
The FRA fixes Alpha's borrowing cost at 7.5% per annum that is the FRA rate for six-month LIBOR of 6.5% plus the100 basis point margin above LIBOR that Alpha will have to pay on its loan. When Alpha obtains the loan after three months, it will pay the lending bank interest at 100 basis points above whatever the current market rate for six-month LIBOR happens to be at the time. Under the FRA agreement, however, there will be a compensating cash payment. Alpha will make a payment to the bank if the fixed FRA rate of 6.5% is higher than the six-month LIBOR rate, and will receive a payment if six-month LIBOR exceeds the fixed FRA rate.

Outcome 1
Suppose that six-month dollar LIBOR on May 4 is 5.75%. Alpha will borrow $10 million at LIBOR plus 100 basis points, 6.75%. The FRA has fixed six-month LIBOR, however, at 6.5%, and Alpha will have to make a compensation payment to the FRA bank for the difference between the FRA rate and actual six-month LIBOR on May 4.

	%
Alpha's loan interest rate (5.75% + 100 basis points)	6.75
Compensation payable by Alpha (6.5 – 5.75)	+ 0.75
All-in borrowing cost with the FRA	7.50

Outcome 2
Suppose that six-month dollar LIBOR on May 4 is 7.75%. Alpha will borrow $10 million for six months at LIBOR plus 100 basis points, 8.75%. The FRA rate of 6.5% is 125 basis points (1.25%) below the

current six-month LIBOR rate, however, and the FRA bank will make a compensating payment to Alpha for the difference.

	%
Alpha's loan interest rate (7.75% + 100 basis points)	8.75
Compensation receivable by Alpha (7.75 – 6.5)	- 1.25
Net borrowing cost with the FRA	7.50

Example 2
Beta expects to make a three-month investment of $10 million, starting in three months' time, and is concerned that interest rates might fall before the investment period begins. The investment yield is expected to be 25 basis points below the three-month LIBOR rate. Beta arranges to sell an FRA to a bank, fixing the three-month LIBOR rate at 6.30%.

Analysis
When Beta makes the investment, it will receive an interest yield of 25 basis points below whatever the three-month LIBOR rate is at that time. However, the FRA has fixed Beta's effective yield at 25 basis points below the FRA rate of 6.30%, i.e. at 6.05% per annum.

For example, suppose that at the start of the investment period, the three-month LIBOR rate is 5.0%. Beta would invest $10 million for three months at 4.75% (5% minus 25 basis points). Under the FRA agreement, however, Beta would receive a compensating payment from the FRA bank for the 130 basis-point difference between the FRA rate of 6.30% and the current LIBOR rate of 5.00%. This will produce an all-in effective yield for Beta of 6.05% per annum.

	%
Beta's investment yield (5.00% - 25 basis points)	4.75
Compensation receivable by Beta (6.30 – 5.00)	+ 1.30
All-in investment yield, with the FRA	6.05

Terms and Terminology

An FRA agreement must specify the notional principal amount, the date from which the interest rate is to be fixed, the settlement date of the FRA, and the notional lending term. The FRA bank will provide the fixed rate at which it will make the transaction.

FRAs are described by the start date (settlement date) and end date of the notional interest term. Terminology for FRAs is not standardized, and there are several ways of describing the period they cover. An FRA that covers a six-month interest-rate period starting in three months' time might be referred to in any of the following ways

- three against nine months
- 3 v 9
- three on nine
- threes, nines
- three over nines.

The notional lending period starts after three months and ends after nine months, giving a notional lending period of six months.

The most common FRA periods are listed below, but periods can be arranged to suit a customer's requirements and the FRA bank will quote a fixed rate accordingly.

1 v 3	1 v 6	2 v 5	2 v 6	3 v 6	3 v 9	3 v 12
6 v 12	6 v 18	9 v 12	9 v 15	9 v 18	12 v 18	12 v 24

If the terms of an FRA agreement are described, for example, as 6.2% on $15 million for 2 v 5, this would mean that the FRA fixes the interest rate at 6.2% per annum for a notional principal amount of $15 million, and for a three-month notional loan period starting in two months' time.

The Compensating Payment

It is usual for the compensating payment from FRA buyer to seller, or from seller to buyer, to take place at the *start* of the notional interest period. For example, for a 6 v 9 FRA, the settlement date when the compensating payment is made will be the end of month 6, not at the end of month 9. The amount of the payment should provide compensation for the difference between the FRA rate and the current market rate on settlement date.

Example

The terms of an FRA are 5.50% on $4 million for 6 v 9. On settlement date at the end of month 6, three-month LIBOR is 7.0%.

Analysis

LIBOR is higher than the FRA rate so a compensating payment will be made by the FRA seller to the FRA buyer. In principle, the amount payable in this example should be for the 1.50% difference between actual LIBOR and the FRA rate, applied to the $4 million principal for a three-month term - i.e. $15,000 (1.5% x $4 million x 3/12). In fact the payment will be less than this because it is made at the start of the interest-rate period (month 6) rather than at the end of the period (month 9).

The $15,000 interest difference is discounted to a lower present value to allow for the early payment.

FRAs as a Hedge

FRAs are a hedging instrument that can remove the uncertainty about future interest costs or yields. They can protect future borrowers against rising interest rates and future lenders and investors against falling rates.

What Amount of Principal can be Hedged?

FRAs can be transacted in any freely traded currency such as dollars, euros, sterling, yen and Swiss francs. The biggest market is dollars. Typical transaction sizes are in the range $1.5 million to $15 million, although they can be arranged for larger amounts.

Duration of the Cover

FRAs are a short-term hedging instrument that can be used to fix interest rates on future loans or investments typically with a starting date of up to 12 months ahead and a notional loan term of up to one year. Very occasionally they might be available for longer maturities, but companies seeking to fix a long-term interest rate would have to consider other hedging instruments such as swaps.

What do FRAs Cost?

FRAs do not have a cost, in the sense that no arrangement fee is payable to the FRA bank that makes a profit from the spread between the rates at which it will buy and sell FRAs. A hidden cost of an FRA, however, like any other contractually binding hedging instrument, is that the interest rate is fixed by the FRA agreement and neither party can benefit from any favorable movement in interest rates. For example, having fixed a borrowing rate by purchasing an FRA, a company is committed to that rate, even if market rates of interest fall.

What Fixed Rates are Available?

FRA rates are quoted by banks that are willing to make such transactions with customers. There is an offer price at which the bank will sell, for customers wishing to buy an FRA to fix a borrowing rate. There is also a lower bid price at which the bank will buy, for customers wishing to sell an FRA to fix a minimum investment yield. The spread between the two rates typically is between three and 10 basis points (0.03%-0.10%).

Different rates are quoted, according to:

● the currency
● the length of the notional interest period, and
● the length of time to the start of the notional interest period.

Rates are based on current market rates of interest at the time the FRA is transacted. For a 3 v 9 FRA in sterling, for example, the fixed bid and offer rates would be based on the forward/forward rate for the six-month period covering the end of month 3 to the end of month 9.

The FRA bank will adjust its quoted prices for its bid-offer spread according to conditions in the market.

How Flexible are FRAs?

An advantage of FRAs is that they are over-the-counter agreements that can be tailored to the specific requirements of the customer with respect to:

- the amount of notional principal
- the timing of the start of the notional interest period (the FRA's settlement date) and
- the duration of the notional interest period.

A company can create an exact hedge for its interest-rate exposures for both amount and timing, but only if it can predict these accurately.

There are also disadvantages associated with FRAs. Because they are OTC agreements, they cannot be resold in a secondary market if the buyer no longer wishes to use the instrument, or wishes to alter the settlement date. In this respect, they lack the flexibility advantage of short-term interest-rate futures.

Strip of FRAs

A strip of FRAs is a series of FRAs, bought or sold at the same time to cover sequential notional interest periods for up to two years or so ahead. The settlement date of each FRA can be timed to coincide with the rollover date on a variable-rate loan or investment, thereby fixing a rate now for each rollover date. A strip of FRAs can be particularly useful, in contrast to a single FRA covering the entire time period, when the amount of the loan or investment changes from one rollover date to the next.

Example

Gamma has borrowed $20 million at a variable rate with six-monthly rollover dates. The loan will be repaid in equal instalments of $5 million at the end of each six-month period, the first instalment due in six months' time. Gamma is concerned about the possibility of rising interest rates, and wishes to use a strip of FRAs to lock in the fixed rates.

A bank quotes the following rates:

6 v 12	6.25%
12 v 18	6.95%
18 v 24	7.10%

Analysis
The interest payable for the first six months has already been fixed, but buying a strip of three FRAs (6 v 12, 12 v 18 and 18 v 24) can be used to lock in interest rates from the end of month 6 up to the maturity of the loan, as follows.

FRA %	Notional principal	Term	Rate
1	$15 million	6 v 12	6.25
2	$10 million	12 v 18	6.95
3	$5 million	18 v 24	7.10

Each FRA in the strip has a different fixed rate. The average rate that the three FRAs has locked in can be calculated as 6.725% per annum, a weighted average rate based on the notional principal borrowed in each six-month period.

Summary

FRAs are one of several derivatives for locking in interest rates and hedging exposures. The risk is limited to failure of the counterparty to make the compensatory payment. They can be described as over-the-counter versions of interest-rate futures, or as short-term swaps because they can convert variable-rate short-term loans or investments into fixed rate.

They do not affect a user's cash flows immediately because no front-end fee is payable and the first cash payment or cash receipt occurs on settlement date, at the start of the loan or investment period.

Their main disadvantages are that:

- they are not readily tradable
- they are binding agreements, unlike options
- they are instruments for short-term hedging only.

Companies seeking a hedge for interest-rate exposures might decide to use futures, options or swaps as an alternative, depending upon their precise needs.

Interest-Rate Futures

A future is a standardized exchange-traded contract for the purchase and sale of an underlying item at an agreed price for settlement on a specified delivery date at some time in the future. A future is a type of forward contract or forward-rate agreement. However, there are several characteristics that distinguish futures from tailor-made, over-the-counter forward contracts.

- A future is an exchange-traded contract. There are a number of futures exchanges around the world, each trading specific contracts for a variety of underlying items.
- It is a contract to buy or sell a standard quantity of a specific item. Several contracts must be traded to buy or sell more than this standard quantity.
- Settlement/delivery date is at a time specified by the exchange authorities. A futures exchange has a number of settlement dates each year, and trading takes place in contracts with March, June, September and December settlement dates.
- A buyer of a future can cancel an obligation to buy for example by closing out a position, at any time before delivery/settlement date, or by selling matching quantities of the same future at the available market price. Similarly, the seller of a future can cancel a contractual obligation at any time before delivery/settlement date by purchasing a matching future at the available market price.

The Purpose of Futures

A futures contract can be used to hedge exposures to risk, to speculate or to exploit arbitrage opportunities. It is a hedging instrument because it can fix a price now for a future transaction in the underlying item, and so remove price uncertainty in the period up to the transaction date. The market price of a future normally will track quite closely the cash market price in the underlying instrument. The difference between the futures price and the cash market price of the underlying item is known as basis. The futures price normally is higher than the cash market price, but the size of the basis reduces over time towards zero. When a futures contract reaches its settlement date, the futures price and the cash market price of the underlying item should be equal, i.e. basis should be zero. A close relationship between the futures price and the cash market price is necessary if futures are to be an effective hedging instrument for price risk.

A future also can be a speculative instrument, because the buyer or seller of a future is not required to buy or sell the underlying item. Instead, futures can be bought and sold in the hope of making a profit from favorable movements in the market price up to delivery/settlement date for the contract.

Short-Term and Long-Term Interest-Rate Futures

Financial futures are contracts for which the underlying item is a financial instrument, and there are financial futures for interest rates, currency exchange rates, share-price indices, and even for the shares of some large individual companies. *Interest-rate* futures can be grouped into two broad types: short-term interest-rate futures (STIRs or shorts) and long-term interest-rate futures (bond futures).

The underlying item of a short-term interest-rate future is a notional money-market deposit of a standard amount and specified term, typically a three-month deposit, or a standard quantity of money-market instruments, e.g. $1 million of 91-day Treasury bills. The futures market price reflects an interest rate for the deposit or the money-market instruments, and selling or buying short-term interest-rate futures at an agreed price locks in an interest rate for the notional amount of funds.

The underlying item for a long-term interest-rate future is a standard quantity of notional government bonds. An example of a bond future traded on the London International Financial Futures Exchange (LIFFE), is the long gilt contract for which the underlying item is £100,000 (nominal value) of notional 7% UK government bonds (gilts). The Eurex futures exchange trades a bond future for which the underlying item is €100,000 (nominal value) of notional 6% German government bonds (Bunds). The futures market price reflects prices in the underlying bond markets that in turn reflect interest yields on long-term government bond investments.

Pricing of Interest-Rate Futures
Short-term interest-rate futures are quoted as an interest rate, but at a discount to a par value of 100. A price of 94.00, for example, represents an interest rate for the underlying deposit of 6% per annum (100 - 94.00 = 6.00). Similarly, a price of 92.00 represents an interest rate of 8% (100 - 92.00 = 8.00). Lower futures prices mean higher short-term interest rates. Prices are quoted to one hundredth of 1% (0.01%) so that a price of 92.75, for example, represents an interest rate of 7.25% (100 - 92.75). The minimum price movement or *tick* for a short-term interest-rate future is either 0.01, i.e. 0.01%, or 0.005, depending on the specifications for the particular futures contract.

Prices for long-term interest-rate futures are quoted in a similar way to bond prices. Bonds are quoted at a price per 100 nominal value, such as $98 per $100 nominal value of Treasury bonds, £96 per £100 nominal value of UK gilts and €102 per €100 nominal value of German government bonds or French government bonds, etc.

For US Treasury bond futures, prices are quoted to one-thirty second of one per cent (1/32 of 1%). A price for US Treasury bond futures of 97 - 16, for example, would mean $97½ per $100 nominal value of bonds (97 + 16/32) and a price of 102 - 24 would mean $102¾ per $100 nominal value (102 + 24/32).

The minimum price movement (tick size) for US bond futures also is one thirty second of one per cent. All other bond futures are priced, like short-term interest-rate futures, to one hundredth of one per cent, e.g. 95.65, and a tick size is 0.01.

Although bond futures prices are similar to prices in the cash markets for bonds, they also reflect long-term interest rates to investors in government bonds. As an approximate guide, the investment yield on a long-term bond is

$$\frac{C}{V} \times 100$$

where

C is the coupon interest rate for the bond, and
V is the market price.

The approximate yield on a long-term bond with a coupon interest rate of 8% and a market price of 96 therefore is 8.33% (8 x 100/96).

Price Changes, and Profits or Losses on Futures Positions
An individual transaction to buy or sell a futures contract for a specified delivery date is made at an agreed price that is the market price at the time of the transaction. The market price of contracts for the same delivery date will move up or down until the last trading day before delivery for the contract.

The market price of interest-rate futures will change as interest rates go up or down.

- If interest rates rise, the market price of interest-rate futures will fall.
- If interest rates fall, the market price of interest-rate futures will rise.

The value of a price change is calculated from the number of ticks of price movement multiplied by the value per tick. The value per tick varies for each futures contract, but is a constant value for the particular contract, at any price level. Price changes are described in terms of ticks. For example, the short sterling future might fall in price on a particular day by 12 ticks, meaning by 0.12. The amount of the profit or loss arising on a person's position in the futures is calculated simply as the number of ticks of price movement, multiplied by the value per tick, multiplied by the number of contracts in the position.

For some of the major futures contracts, tick values are shown in the table below.

Short-term interest-rate futures	Exchange	Notional deposit per contract	Tick size %	Value per tick
3-month eurodollar	CME	$1 million	0.01	$25
13-week Treasury bills	CME	$1 million	0.005	$12.50
3-month (short) sterling	LIFFE	£500,000	0.01	£12.50
3-month euribor	LIFFE	€1 million	0.005	€12.50
3-month euroswiss	LIFFE	SF1 million	0.01	SF 25
3-month euroyen	LIFFE	¥100 million	0.005	¥1,250

Bond future	Exchange	Contract size (bond nominal value)	Tick size %	Value per tick
Long gilt (British government bonds)	LIFFE	£100,000	0.01	£10
Bund (German government bonds)	EUREX	€100,000	0.01	€10
US Treasury bond	CBOT	$100,000	1/32	$31.25

The value per tick of a three-month eurodollar contract, for example, is 0.01% on the underlying notional deposit of $1 million for three months that is $25 (0.0001 x $1 million x 3/12). Similarly, the value per tick for a three-month sterling contract is 0.01% on the underlying deposit of £500,000 for three months that is £12.50 (0.0001 x £500,000 x 3/12).

Buying and Selling Short-Term Interest-Rate Futures

The buyer of a short-term interest-rate futures contract at a fixed price is buying future interest income on the underlying notional deposit at an agreed rate of interest. If market rates of interest go up and the futures price falls, the buyer suffers a loss because the yield that has been fixed by purchasing the future is less than the yield obtainable at the current market rate.

The seller of a futures contract is agreeing to borrow a notional deposit at a fixed rate of interest. If market interest rates go up and the futures price falls, the seller will benefit because the fixed borrowing rate is less than the current market rate payable.

- The buyer of a futures contract at an agreed price will therefore make a profit at the expense of the seller if the market price goes up. On the other hand, the buyer will make a loss if the market price goes down.
- Similarly, the seller of a futures contract at an agreed price will make a profit at the expense of the buyer if the market price falls, but a loss if the market price goes up.

The profit or loss for the buyer of a futures contract matches the loss or profit for the seller. The amount of the profit or loss for each futures contract bought or sold is the number of ticks of price change multiplied by the value per tick.

Example

Alpha sold 10 June short sterling futures at a price of 93.15. The price of June short sterling futures subsequently fell to 93.00.

Analysis

The price has fallen by 15 ticks per contract. Alpha, as a seller of the futures, therefore has made a profit of £1,875 (10 contracts x 15 ticks per contract x £12.50 per tick).

Long and Short Positions

Futures can be sold as well as bought. It might seem odd that someone should be able to sell something that he/she does not have, but this is a feature of trading in any instrument for a forward delivery/settlement date. A person who sells an item for forward delivery/settlement, who does not yet own the item, is said to be going short in the item.

When futures are first bought or sold, the buyer or seller is said to have an open position. A buyer has a long position in the contract and a seller has a short position.

For example, if a bank that has not previously traded in December eurodollar futures, buys 20 contracts, it becomes long in December eurodollar futures by 20 contracts. Similarly, a person who sells 50 March Bund futures without having previously purchased any is said to be short in March Bund futures by 50 contracts.

Closing Positions

A position normally is closed before the futures contracts reach delivery/settlement.

- A buyer can close a long position by selling an equal number of contracts for the same delivery date, thus reversing the original purchase transaction.
- A seller can close an open position by purchasing an equal number of contracts for the same delivery date, thus reversing the original sale transaction.

On closing a position, there will be an overall profit or loss on trading, depending on whether the sale price is higher than the purchase price or vice versa.

Example
Bravo sells 40 September three-month short sterling contracts on LIFFE

on 16 July at a price of 95.90, and subsequently closes the position on 10 September by purchasing 40 September contracts at a price of 94.64.

Analysis
Bravo makes a profit of 126 ticks per contract (95.90 - 94.64 = 1.26) on closing the position. The total profit on trading in the futures has been £63,000 (40 contracts x 126 ticks x £12.50 per tick). This profit will be paid to Bravo in cash from the exchange via Bravo's broker, although Bravo could have withdrawn some of this profit earlier because profits or losses are monitored and individual positions are marked-to-market daily.

The ability to close a position at any time gives futures contracts a valuable flexibility as to timing. The buyer or seller does not have to wait until a contract reaches its delivery date to realize any profit or loss.

Delivery

Occasionally, the holder of a position in futures will not close the position but will let the contract run to delivery. Futures contracts that reach delivery are settled either by:

- cash settlement, or
- physical delivery.

Profits or losses are calculated for cash settlement as for closing a position before delivery, except that the final price at the delivery date, the Exchange Delivery Settlement Price, is used as the closing buying or selling price to measure the profit or loss on a position. All short-term interest-rate futures are cash-settled on delivery.

For physical delivery of the underlying item, the seller delivers the item to the buyer who pays a purchase price in exchange. Bond futures are settled by physical delivery. The underlying instrument for bond futures is a quantity of notional bonds, and when the buyer takes physical delivery, the seller must provide equivalent bonds from a list that the exchange has specified as suitable.

Hedging with Short-Term Interest-Rate Futures

Futures can be used to hedge an exposure to a rise or fall in short-term interest rates over a period of up to approximately two years. However, most futures trading is in contracts with near delivery dates, and hedging with futures is principally against the risk of adverse movements in interest rates over a period of up to the next six months.

- A company expecting to borrow can lock in an interest rate by selling futures. If interest rates go up, the price of the future will fall, and the company will make a profit on its futures hedge to offset the loss it suffers due to the higher interest rate.
- A company expecting to lend or invest can lock in an interest yield by buying futures. If interest rates fall, the price of the future will rise and the company will make a profit on its futures hedge, to offset the loss it suffers due to the lower interest rate.

Several contracts will have to be bought or sold to hedge an exposure in full. For example, to hedge an exposure of $20 million to the risk of an increase in interest rates, it would be necessary to sell 20 eurodollar future contracts or 20 US Treasury bill contracts.

A hedge is obtained in a similar way to FRAs. The underlying item for short-term interest rate futures is a notional deposit, and buyers and sellers are trading in the price of short-term deposits, i.e. in interest rates, independently from the loan or investment.

If a company at the beginning of January expects to borrow £500,000 for three months from mid-February, and wishes to hedge against the risk of an increase in interest rates, it can sell one March three-month sterling future and close its position in mid-February when the loan is obtained. The loan will be arranged at the current market rate. There will be a profit or a loss, however, on closing the futures position. Taking this profit or loss together with the actual cost of the loan, the net cost to the company will be the interest rate fixed by the original sale of the future.

The profit or loss on the future therefore is comparable to the compensatory payment with an FRA.

Example 1

Echo expects to borrow $25 million for three months, starting in two months' time in early June, and expects to pay interest at three-month dollar LIBOR plus 50 basis points. It wishes to use eurodollar futures to hedge the exposure to rising interest rates. It sells 25 June eurodollar contracts ($25 million ÷ $1 million per contract) at a price of 94.40. Echo subsequently closes the position in early June at a price of 93.70, when it also borrows $25 million at 6.80%, the current three-month US dollar LIBOR rate of 6.30% plus 0.50 basis points.

Analysis

By selling five eurodollar futures at 94.40, Echo has locked in a rate of 5.60% (100 - 94.40) for LIBOR for its $25 million loan. Borrowing at LIBOR plus 50 basis points, this will lock in a total rate of 6.10%.

A three-month loan of $25 million at 6.10% would have an interest cost of about $381,250 ($25 million x 6.10% x 3/12).

In effect, Echo borrows at 6.80% and will pay interest of $425,000 on its loan ($25 million x 6.80% x 3/12). However, there is a profit on its futures position.

Original sale price per contract	94.40
Purchase price on closing position	93.70
Profit per contract	0.70
	= 70 ticks
Total profit for 25 contracts	= 25 contracts x 70 ticks x $25 per tick
	= $43,750

The profit, taken with the actual cost of loan interest, produces a net cost equal to borrowing $25 million for three months at 6.10%, the rate locked in by the original futures transaction.

	$
Actual loan cost (6.80%)	425,000
Profit on futures hedge (70 ticks)	- 43,750
Net loan cost (6.10%)	381,250

Example 2

Foxtrot expects to invest £20 million for three months at LIBOR minus 50 basis points, starting next month in early November, and wishes to use futures to hedge against a fall in interest rates before then. It buys 40 December three-month short sterling futures at a price of 93.10 (40 contracts x £500,000 per contract = £20 million). In early November when it makes the investment, Foxtrot closes the futures position by selling 40 December contracts at 92.80, and invests £20 million for three months at 6.70%, the three-month LIBOR rate of 7.20% minus 50 basis points.

Analysis

By purchasing futures at 93.10, Foxtrot has locked in an interest rate of 6.90% for three-month LIBOR (100 – 93.10) and so has locked in an interest yield on its investment of 6.40%, the fixed rate minus 50 basis points.

The yield from a three-month investment of £20 million at 6.40% could be £320,000 (£20 million x 6.40% x 3/12).

The investment is made at an interest rate of 6.70%, yielding £335,000 (£20 million x 6.70% x 3/12) over the three months. However, Foxtrot has made a loss on its futures position.

Original purchase price per contract	93.10
Sale price on closing position	92.80
Profit per contract	0.30
	= 30 ticks
Total profit for 40 contracts	= 40 contracts x 30 ticks x £12.50 per tick
	= £15,000

This hedging loss taken with the actual yield on the investment produces a net yield equal to investing £20 million for three months at 6.40%, the rate locked in by the original futures transaction.

	£
Actual investment yield (6.70%)	335,000
Loss on futures hedge (30 ticks)	- 15,000
Net investment yield (6.40%)	320,000

Floating Rate Loans and Investments
Short-term interest-rate futures also can be used if required to hedge against interest-rate changes on a floating-rate loan or investment, for successive rollover dates up to about two years ahead, depending on the availability of far-dated futures contracts.

Example
Indigo has a floating rate loan of $10 million with three-monthly rollover dates, on which it pays interest at LIBOR plus 100 basis points. The loan has about 16 months to maturity, and there are four more rollover dates, in May, August and November this year and February next year.

Analysis
Indigo could use futures to lock in an interest rate for each rollover date. It could sell ten three-month eurodollar futures contracts ($10 million ÷ $1 million per contract) for June delivery, a further ten for September delivery, ten for December delivery and ten for delivery in March next year. Suppose the prices obtained were as follows:

Delivery date	Price	Dollar LIBOR interest rates
June	93.40	6.60% (100 – 93.40)
September	93.30	6.70% (100 – 93.30)
December	93.18	6.82% (100 – 93.18)
March	93.05	6.95% (100 – 93.05)

By locking in these rates for three-month dollar LIBOR, Indigo can fix the cost of borrowing by closing the June contract position at the May rollover date, closing the September contract position at the August rollover date, and so on. The interest rate fixed for each successive rollover date (LIBOR plus 100 bp) will be 6.60%, 6.70%, 6.82% and 6.95% respectively.

Hedging for Longer Interest-Rate Maturities

Most short-term interest rate futures have a three-month deposit or money market security as the underlying instrument. Longer interest-rate maturities, for example, a six-month interest rate, also can be fixed by trading in futures. To fix the interest rate in advance for six-month borrowing, it would be necessary to sell two futures contracts for three-month deposits, 6 months ÷ 3 months per contract = 2 contracts. Fixing the rate will be exact only if there is no change in the yield curve, and the spread between interest rates for different maturities remains constant.

Example

Victor expects to borrow £5 million for six months, at six-month LIBOR, starting from the middle of next month (June), and is concerned that interest rates are about to rise. Current rates of interest are 5% for three-month LIBOR and 5.25% for six-month LIBOR. Victor decides to hedge the interest rate risk by selling three-month sterling futures, for which the price is 95.00.

Analysis

Victor wishes to obtain a hedge for six-month borrowing, but short sterling futures are for three-month deposits. Two futures contracts therefore must be sold for each £500,000 principal amount hedged. Victor must sell 20 June contracts at 95.00 (£5 million ÷ £500,000 per contract x 2).

Suppose that when Victor obtains the loan in mid-June and closes its position by purchasing 20 June contracts, three-month LIBOR is 6%, six-month LIBOR is 6.25% and the price for June short sterling futures is 94.00.

The difference between three-month and six-month LIBOR is still 25 basis points (0.25%), the same spread as when the 20 contracts were sold, so Victor has successfully fixed the cost of borrowing at 5.25%, the six-month rate when the futures position was opened.

The interest cost of borrowing £5 million for six months at 5.25% would be £131,250 (£5 million x 5.25% x 6/12).

The actual cost of borrowing in June for six months is 6.25%, at an interest cost of £156,250 (£5 million x 6.25% x 6/12). However, Victor has made a profit on its futures position of 100 ticks per contract.

Original sale price per contract	95.00
Purchase price on closing position	94.00
Profit per contract	1.00
	= 100 ticks
Total profit for 20 contracts	= 20 contracts x 100 ticks x £12.50 per tick
	= £25,000

The profit on futures trading, set against the actual cost of borrowing, results in a net cost equal to the cost of borrowing £5 million for six months at 5.25%.

	£
Actual cost of borrowing (6.25%)	156,250
Profit on futures hedge (100 ticks)	- 25,000
Net borrowing cost (5.25%)	131,250

Hedging with Bond Futures

The market price of long-term bonds goes up when interest rates fall, and down when interest rates rise. An investor in bonds, particularly government bonds, can hedge his exposure to an increase in interest rates by selling bond futures. Similarly, a bank or other company that expects to invest shortly in bonds can hedge its exposure to the risk of interest rates falling before the investment is made, by purchasing bond futures. The effective price for the bonds is then fixed because the profit or loss on futures trading offsets any fall or increase in the market value of the bonds in the period up to closing the futures position, or delivery date for the contracts.

Advantages of Interest-Rate Futures as a Hedging Instrument

Futures are just one method of hedging interest-rate exposures by fixing an interest rate for anticipated short-term borrowing, lending or investing, or by fixing in advance a price or value for bonds. An important advantage of futures as a hedging instrument is the flexibility of closing a position at any time before delivery date, so that the hedge can be timed to match exactly the underlying borrowing, lending or investment transaction. In contrast, the settlement date or exercise date for FRAs and European-style interest-rate options is set for an exact date when the transaction is arranged, giving the user no timing flexibility should the loan or investment date be slightly delayed or brought forward.

The user of futures also has the opportunity to benefit from current market prices, should these seem particularly favorable, by closing a position before the loan or investment takes place.

Example
In April, a company sells September eurodollar futures at 94.00 to fix the interest rate on anticipated borrowings (in mid-September) at 6%. The dollar interest rate subsequently increases to 8%, and in mid-August the futures price is 92.00. The company at this time believes that the interest rate has peaked and might fall during the next few weeks.

Analysis

The company can close its position in mid-August, securing a profit on its futures trading of 200 ticks per contract (94.00 - 92.00). If, as the company expects, the dollar interest rate falls before the company has to borrow in mid-September, to 6.5% for example, the futures price will rise to 93.50. If the company had delayed closing the position its profit would have been less, just 50 ticks per contract in this example. By closing its position early, the effect of the subsequent fall in interest rates would be to reduce the net cost of borrowing below the 6% that the company was originally trying to fix.

Disadvantages of Hedging with Futures

There are also some disadvantages in using futures.

Anyone buying or selling futures is required to pay a cash deposit to the futures exchange. This deposit is known as either margin or performance bond. The purpose of margin is to protect the futures exchange against credit risk in the form of default by the buyer or seller of futures. When two parties make a transaction in futures, the clearing house of the exchange steps in and becomes the counterparty in the transaction to both the buyer and the seller. The exchange becomes the buyer to a seller of futures, and at the same time becomes the seller to the buyer of the futures. If any buyer or seller defaults, it is the exchange that will suffer the loss.

An initial margin is required to cover the exchange against the risk of foreseeable short-term losses on the person's position. If actual losses are incurred, a further payment (variation margin) is required to cover the loss.

Initial margins and variation margins tie up cash in deposits for the sale or purchase transaction until the futures position is closed. Although only a relatively small margin is required to buy or sell a future, for a company buying or selling futures in large quantities, the cumulative cash investment in margins can be quite high.

There can be a considerable amount of administrative work to manage futures positions efficiently. Direct debit arrangements can be established for the payment of margins, but positions in each contract must be monitored continually, and regular decisions taken about opening or closing positions to ensure that the intended interest-rate hedges work effectively.

Futures are a short-term hedging method, and most contracts traded on an exchange are for the next one or two delivery dates. The range of available interest-rate contracts is fairly limited and restricted to the major currencies, and most short-term interest-rate futures are for notional three-month deposits or instruments.

Summary

A significant proportion of futures transactions are carried out for speculation and arbitrage, with a lesser proportion of transactions intended as a hedge. Even so, futures are used extensively for hedging by banks and non-bank companies.

Banks are the biggest users of futures for hedging. Dealing with very large quantities of financial assets and liabilities in different currencies, their interest-rate and currency exposures that arise from their transactions in other markets such as lending and borrowing markets, options markets, FRAs, etc., can be significant. They can hedge their over-the-counter transactions with customers by executing matching trades in futures.

Interest-Rate Options

An interest-rate option is an instrument sold by an option writer to an option holder for a price known as a premium. The option gives its holder the right but not the obligation, on or before a specified expiry date, to:

- borrow a notional quantity of funds for a specified term at a specified, i.e. fixed, rate of interest, or
- lend or deposit a notional quantity of funds for a specified term at a specified interest yield, or
- purchase or sell one interest-rate future at a specified price.

The specified rate of interest for borrowing or lending is the *strike price* or *exercise price* of the option. For options on *futures*, the strike price is the specified purchase or sale price for the underlying future. Options on interest-rate futures are exchange-traded instruments, bought and sold on the same exchange, where the futures are traded. All other interest-rate options are purchased over-the-counter from a bank, on terms negotiated between the bank, the option writer, and the customer.

Over-the-counter (OTC) options are one of the following types:

- borrower's option
- lender's option
- cap
- floor
- collar.

Here we are concerned with the use of options as a hedge for interest-rate exposures, but a brief introductory description of the characteristics of options is provided.

Characteristics of Options

A *call option* gives its holder the right to buy an underlying instrument at the strike price, and obliges the option writer to sell the instrument at that price when and if the option is exercised. A borrower's option and an interest-rate cap are types of OTC call option, giving their holder the right to buy a notional quantity of funds for the cost of the strike price that is a specific interest rate. For example, a borrower's option may give its holder the right to obtain a notional six-month loan of $10 million, starting on 5 May, at an interest rate of 5.75%.

A *put option* gives its holder the right to sell an underlying instrument at the strike price, and obliges the option writer to buy the instrument at that price when and if the option is exercised. A lender's option and an interest-rate floor are types of OTC put option, giving their holder the right to sell (lend or deposit) a notional quantity of funds at the strike price. For example, a lender's option may give its holder the right to make a notional three-month deposit of $10 million, starting at any time up to and including 16th November, at an interest rate of 4.75%.

An option is written for a specified term and has an expiry date. An *American option* can be exercised at any time up to and including its expiry date. A *European option* can be exercised on its expiry date only and not before. If an option is not exercised by its expiry date, the option lapses.

The strike price of an OTC option is for a benchmark or reference interest rate, such as three-month LIBOR or six-month LIBOR. The option gives its holder the right to borrow or lend the notional funds with the reference rate of interest fixed at the strike price. For example, if the strike price of a borrower's option is 6% for six-month LIBOR, the option holder has the right to borrow the notional funds on or before the expiry date at a guaranteed six-month LIBOR rate of 6%.

The strike price of an option can be more favorable to the option holder, less favorable or the same as the current market rate of interest for the reference rate. An option is *in-the-money* if its strike price is more favorable than the current market rate, *out-of-the-money* if it is less favorable and *at-the-money* if the strike price and the current market rate are the same. For example, if a borrower's option has a strike price of 5.5% for three-month LIBOR, and the current market rate for three-month LIBOR is 6.25%, the option is in-the-money because it is cheaper to borrow with LIBOR at the strike price of 5.5% than at the current market rate for LIBOR of 6.25%.

An option can be in-the-money, out-of-the-money or at-the-money *when it is written*, and the strike price is agreed between option buyer and option writer. In-the-money options, however, have a higher premium, and are more expensive to buy than out-of-the-money options. An option will be *exercised* only if it is in-the-money on the exercise/expiry date.

Exercising an Option

When an OTC option is exercised, the option holder takes up the right to borrow or lend the notional quantity of funds for a specified term with the reference interest rate at the strike price. There is no actual loan or deposit, however, and an option is settled by a cash payment from the option writer to the option holder.

For example, suppose that a lender's option has a strike price of 6% for three-month LIBOR, and a notional principal amount of $10 million. On expiry, if the market rate for three-month LIBOR is 4.5%, the option will be exercised because it is more profitable to lend $10 million at the strike price of 6% than at the market rate of 4.5%.

On exercise of the option, there is no transaction of a $10 million loan at 6% interest. Instead, a compensatory payment will be made, based on the difference of 150 basis points (6.00% - 4.50%) between the strike price and the LIBOR market rate. The difference is applied to the notional principal of $10 million for the term of the notional loan as specified in the option agreement, in this example, probably for a three-month period because the reference rate is three-month LIBOR.

In the case of borrowers' and lenders' options, the compensatory payment is made immediately when the option is exercised. For caps, floors and collars the compensatory payment does not take place until the end of the interest-rate period to which it relates.

Options as a Hedge

An option can be used to hedge an interest-rate exposure by locking in a worst-case interest rate for borrowing or lending/investing. Without the option, the borrower or lender would be at risk from a rise or fall in the general level of interest rates. The option provides interest-rate protection, and at the same time allows the option holder to benefit from a favorable change in the market rate. If an option is out-of-the-money on expiry, it will be allowed to lapse, and the option holder can borrow or lend at the lower or higher available market rate. The cost of this interest-rate protection is the premium payable for the option.

Because an option will be used only in circumstances where it benefits the option holder, it can be described as a conditional hedging instrument. This is distinct from binding contracts such as FRAs and futures that can be described as *outright* hedging instruments.

Hedging with a Borrower's Option

A borrower's option can be used to secure a maximum effective interest rate for future short-term borrowing while allowing the option holder to benefit from lower market rates of interest if these are available when the loan is eventually transacted.

Example
Alpha has to borrow $20 million for six months in two months' time. It expects to be offered an interest rate of six-month dollar LIBOR + 75

its by its bank. Six-month dollar LIBOR is 6%, and Alpha does
to pay more than 7.75% in interest.

Alpha decides to buy a European-style borrower's option from the bank
at a strike price of 6.5% for six-month LIBOR for a notional principal
amount of $20 million and with an expiry date in two months, scheduled
to coincide with the start of the loan period. The premium cost of
$50,000 represents an interest cost equivalent of 50 basis points, 0.50%
per annum on the notional principal amount for the six-month period.

Analysis
Alpha expects to borrow at LIBOR plus 75 basis points, but does not
want to pay an effective rate in excess of 7.75%. The effective interest
rate includes the cost of the premium, that for a borrower's option at a
strike price of 6.5%, is 0.50% per annum.

A strike price of 6.5% would secure a maximum borrowing cost of
7.75%, as follows:

	%
Premium cost (interest equivalent)	0.50
Strike price	6.50
Excess of borrowing rate over LIBOR	0.75
All-in maximum borrowing cost	7.75

Outcome 1
On the expiry date, if six-month LIBOR is 8%, higher than the strike
price, the borrower's option will be exercised. Alpha will borrow
$20 million for six months at 8.75%, the current LIBOR rate plus
75 basis points. However, the bank, the option writer, will make a
compensatory payment equivalent to the different between the strike
price (6.5%) and the current market rate (8%). The effective cost of
borrowing will be as follows:

	%
Premium cost (interest equivalent)	0.50
Loan at LIBOR plus 75 basis points	8.75
Less: Compensatory payment	- 1.50
All-in borrowing cost	7.75

Outcome 2

On the expiry date, if six-month LIBOR is 5.5%, below the strike price, the borrower's option will be allowed to lapse. Alpha will borrow $20 million at 6.25% LIBOR plus 75 basis points. The effective borrowing cost, including the premium for the option, will be 6.75%.

	%
Premium cost (interest equivalent)	0.50
Loan at LIBOR plus 75 basis points	6.25
All-in borrowing cost	6.75

Whatever the market rate for LIBOR on expiry of the option, the effective borrowing cost for Alpha will not exceed 7.75%. If interest rates are below the strike price for the option, and the option is not exercised, the effective borrowing cost will be less than 7.75%, and Alpha will have paid a premium for an unused option. The premium might be described as the cost of an interest-rate insurance policy.

Hedging with a Lender's Option

A lender's option can be used to secure a minimum effective interest yield on future short-term lending or investment while allowing the option holder to benefit from higher market rates of interest, if these are available when the loan or investment is eventually made.

Example

Beta expects to invest $20 million in one month's time for a period of three months, but is anxious about the possibility that interest rates will soon fall. It expects to deposit the funds at three-month LIBOR minus 50 basis points. Three-month LIBOR is 7%, and Beta would like to ensure that its minimum yield is 5.25%. A lender's option on a notional three-month deposit of $20 million at a strike price of 6% would have a premium cost of $12,500, equivalent to an interest cost of 0.25 basis points, 0.25% per annum on the notional principal amount, for a three-month period.

Analysis

Beta expects to invest at LIBOR minus 50 basis points, but wants to secure a minimum yield of 5.25%. The effective interest yield for Beta is calculated after deducting the premium cost. A strike price of 6% would give Beta the following minimum yield.

	%
Strike rate	6.00
Rate below LIBOR for investing	- 0.50
Premium cost (interest equivalent)	- 0.25
All-in borrowing cost	5.25

On the expiry date, if three month LIBOR is lower than 6%, at 5.5% for example, the option will be exercised and Beta will secure the minimum yield of 5.25%. Beta would invest at 5.0%, current LIBOR minus 50 basis points, but would receive a compensatory payment from the bank (option writer) for the difference between three-month LIBOR and the strike price.

	%
Investment rate (5.50 – 0.50)	5.00
Compensatory payment received (6.0 – 5.50)	+ 0.50
Less: premium cost (interest equivalent)	- 0.25
All-in borrowing cost	5.25

On the expiry date, if three-month LIBOR is higher than the strike price, for example 6.875%, the lender's option will be allowed to lapse. Beta will invest $20 million for three months at LIBOR minus 50 basis points (6.375%) and the effective net yield after deducting the premium cost of 0.25% will be 6.125%.

	%
Investment rate (6.875 – 0.50)	6.375
Less: premium cost (interest equivalent)	- 0.250
All-in borrowing cost	6.125

The effective net yield for Beta will be a minimum of 5.25%, and higher if the option is not exercised when the market rate for investing or lending exceeds the strike price. As with a borrower's option, the premium for a lender's option can be described as the cost of an insurance policy that the option holder would prefer not to use.

Hedging with Interest-Rate Caps

An interest-rate cap is an agreement giving its buyer a series of borrowers' options setting a maximum interest rate on variable-rate borrowing. Under a cap agreement, the seller (writer) agrees to compensate the buyer (holder) if interest rates rise above the strike price at each reset date (rollover date) for the loan. A cap can be arranged for just one reset date, in which case it would be a borrower's option, or for a whole series of rollover dates. The term of a cap can range from three months up to 12 years, but most are between two and five years.

The cap buyer pays the seller a premium, normally up-front when the transaction is made. The terms of a cap can be structured to the customer's requirements for strike price, maturity and rollover dates and can match the maturity and rollover dates for the underlying floating-rate loan.

The purpose of a cap is to provide its holder with protection from adverse movements in interest rates by setting a maximum borrowing cost for any rollover date on a variable-rate loan. At the same time, the holder has the flexibility to take advantage of lower market rates of interest when they occur.

Although a cap is used to provide a hedge against an increase in interest rates on an underlying loan, it is, like a borrower's option, a completely separate transaction from the loan itself. The cap is for a notional principal amount that is likely to be several million dollars, or an equivalent amount in another currency. Some banks, however, will sell caps for smaller notional amounts. The reference interest rate for the strike price normally is three-month or six-month LIBOR for dollars and sterling although another reference rate such as one-month LIBOR, a

US Treasury bill rate or a commercial rate could be used, and the three-month or six-month euribor rate for euros.

A borrower's option requires the option holder to notify the option writer of his intention to exercise the option, and there is a compensatory payment on exercise at the beginning of the interest-rate period to which the option relates. In contrast, for a cap, each option is automatically exercised on a rollover date when the market rate of interest is higher than the strike price. However, the compensatory payment by the cap writer to the cap holder does not occur until the end of the interest-rate period to which the option relates, typically three or six months later.

Example

Gamma is arranging a three-year floating-rate loan of £10 million with six-monthly rollover dates. Interest is payable at six-month LIBOR plus 100 basis points. Six-month LIBOR is 5%, and Gamma wishes to buy a cap to ensure that interest payable does not exceed 7% at any rollover date, ignoring the cost of the cap premium. The premium for a three-year cap at a strike price of 6% for six-month LIBOR would be £150,000.

During the term of the loan and the cap, six-month LIBOR was as follows:

Six-month LIBOR

	%
Start of loan/cap period	5.0
After 6 months	6.5
After 1 year	4.5
After 1½ years	6.0
After 2 years	6.5
After 2½ years	7.0

The strike price of 6% for six-month LIBOR ensures that Gamma, paying interest at LIBOR plus 100 basis points, will not pay more than

7% for any rollover period on the loan, ignoring the cap premium cost. The cap writer will make a compensatory payment whenever six-month LIBOR exceeds 6% on a rollover date.

Suppose that actual interest rates over the cap period are as follows:

Interest period	Interest rate for next six months (LIBOR + 100 bp)	Amount of compensation (interest equivalent)	Net loan cost
	%	%	%
6 months-1 year	7.5	0.5	7.0
1 year-1½ years	5.5	None	5.5
1½ years-2 years	7.0	None	7.0
2 years-2½ years	7.5	0.5	7.0
2½ years-3 years	8.0	1.0	7.0

Compensation would be about £25,000 (0.5% of £10 million x 6/12) at the end of the first year and after 2½ years, and £50,000 (1% of £10 million x 6/12) for the final rollover period, payable at the end of the loan term.

In this example, because the cap premium was £150,000, Gamma has paid in premium more than the compensatory payments received, and so can be said to have made a loss on the hedge. However, Gamma had the security of knowing that the interest rates payable would not exceed 7% net for three years, and also the flexibility to take advantage of lower interest rates; in this example at the rollover date after one year when LIBOR was down to 4.5%.

Hedging with Interest-Rate Floors

An interest-rate floor is comparable to a cap in the same way that a lender's option can be compared to a borrower's option. It is a series of lenders' options that sets a minimum interest yield on a variable-rate investment or loan to a customer. The floor buyer pays a premium to the writer (seller); in return, the writer agrees to compensate the buyer if interest rates fall below the strike price at each reset date for the investment or loan. As with a cap, the terms of a floor agreement can be tailored to the requirements of the customer for strike price, interest reference rate, rollover dates and maturity.

A floor can provide a hedge against falling interest rates, and fix a minimum interest yield for a lender or investor, while at the same time giving the holder the flexibility to benefit from higher market rates of interest when these occur.

Example

Delta is arranging a two-year investment of $20 million, on which interest receivable will be 75 basis points below three-month dollar LIBOR. Rollover dates will be every three months. Three-month dollar LIBOR is 6.5%, and Delta does not want its interest yield to be less than 5% at any rollover date on the investment.

For a premium of $280,000, Delta could buy a floor with a notional principal of $20 million and a strike price of 6%. For interest-rate caps and floors, available strike prices are in whole percentage figures.

Analysis

A strike price of 6% will fix the minimum interest yield for any rollover period on the investment at 5.25% (6% - 75 basis points). Suppose, for example, that three-month LIBOR is 6.5% at the start of the investment and then 6%, 5%, 4.75%, 4%, 4.25, 7% and 8% at the subsequent three-monthly rollover dates on the investment.

Delta's net income would be as follows:

Interest period	Interest rate for next three (LIBOR minus 75bp) %	Amount of compensation (interest equivalent) %	Net yield %
3 months – 6 months	5.25	None	5.25
6 months – 9 months	4.25	1.00	5.25
9 months – 12 months	4.00	1.25	5.25
12 months – 15 months	3.25	2.00	5.25
15 months – 18 months	3.50	1.75	5.25
18 months – 21 months	6.25	None	6.25
21 months – 24 months	7.25	None	7.25

Delta would receive the following compensation payments, approximate calculations, at the end of the relevant interest-rate period.

End of month		Compensation $
9	($20 million x 1% x 3/12)	50,000
12	($20 million x 1.25% x 3/12)	62,500
15	($20 million x 2% x 3/12)	100,000
18	($20 million x 1.75% x 3/12)	87,500

In this example, because the floor premium was $280,000, Delta could be said to have made a profit on the hedge. More significantly, however, Delta also has had the risk protection of a guaranteed minimum yield over the two-year period. It also has been able to benefit from higher interest rates at the end of months 18 and 21.

Hedging with Interest-Rate Collars

A major disadvantage of caps and floors as hedge for interest-rate exposures is their high cost. Premiums typically range from 100 to 500 basis points of the notional principal, and are payable up-front. Collars were devised as a lower-cost alternative to caps and floors. A collar is a combination of buying a cap and selling a floor, or buying a floor and selling a cap.

A company wishing to fix a maximum interest-rate cost for a variable-rate loan and at the same time wanting some flexibility to benefit from more favorable interest rates when they occur, could transact a collar with a bank in which it:

- buys a cap with a strike price at the required maximum limit
- simultaneously sells a floor to the bank at a lower strike price, for the same maturity and notional principal.

The net premium is the cost of the premium payable for the cap minus the premium receivable for selling the floor.

For example, a company might arrange a five-year collar on notional principal of $25 million, setting a strike rate of 7% for the cap limit, and a strike rate of 5% for the floor rate. In effect, the collar consists of buying a cap with a strike rate of 7% and selling a floor with a strike rate of 5%. The collar means that the effective LIBOR rate paid by the company will never exceed 7% but will never fall below 5%.

The effect of a collar is to set both a maximum and a minimum interest rate on the borrowing. If interest rates rise above the cap strike price, the collar holder will receive compensation, but if interest rates fall below the floor strike price, the collar holder must pay compensation to the bank. This limits the flexibility to benefit from lower interest rates, but in return the net premium is lower.

Similarly, a company wishing to fix a minimum interest yield for a floating-rate investment while retaining some flexibility to benefit from higher market rates of interest should they occur, could transact a collar in which it:

- buys a floor with a strike price at the required minimum level, and
- simultaneously sells a cap to the bank at a higher strike price.

The net premium is the premium payable for the floor minus the premium receivable for selling the cap. The effect of the collar would be to fix a minimum interest yield with the floor's strike price, but limit the maximum yield obtainable, in the event that market interest rates rise, to the cap strike price level.

In choosing between a cap or floor and a collar, a company must balance the lower cost of the premium for the collar against the limited flexibility to benefit from favorable movements in interest rates. Both a cap or floor and a collar, however, provide the required interest-rate protection against adverse rate movements.

Delta Hedging

Institutions that trade options, i.e. write options, are exposed to the risk of losses from an adverse change in the price of the underlying instrument or item. Traders in interest-rate options for example, are exposed to the risk of an adverse movement in the underlying interest rate. This risk can be offset by delta hedging.

Delta

Delta is a measure of the rate of change in the premium value of an option, with respect to a change in the current price of the underlying item. For call options, delta can range from a value of 0 to a value of $+1$. For put options, the value of the delta can range from -1 to 0.

When a call option is at-the-money, i.e. when the strike price of the option is the same as the price of the underlying item, the delta of the option will be 0.5. A call option that is deeply in-the-money has a delta approaching $+1$. A call option that is deeply out-of-the-money has a delta of 0.

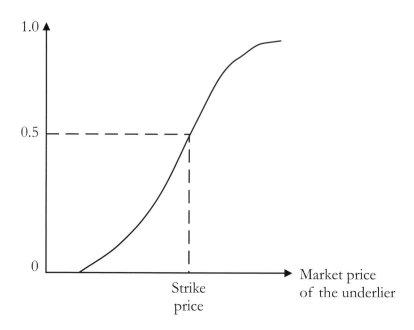

Delta of a Call

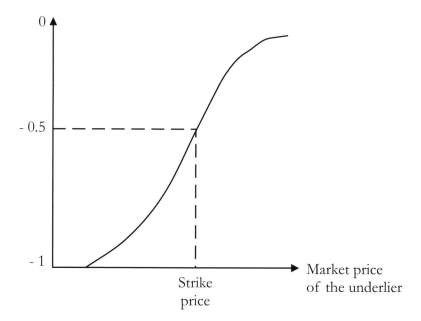

Delta of a Put

Suppose that a borrower's option on twelve-month LIBOR has a strike price of 6% and the cash market LIBOR rate is 8%. The delta of the option will be 0.5. Let's presume that the market price of the option is 2.4 basis points, i.e. $0.024 per $1 of notional principal. An increase in the market rate of interest from 6% to 6.1%, an increase of 10 basis points, should result in the value of the option rising by 5 basis points, the rise in the cash market price multiplied by the delta of the option. The price of the option should rise from 2.4 basis points to 7.4 basis points. This would represent a loss to the option writer and a gain to the option holder.

What is Delta Hedging?

To eliminate risk from option trading, a trader can create a delta hedge in order to create delta neutrality.

- An option on bonds typically is hedged by buying or selling bonds.

- An option on futures typically is hedged by buying or selling futures.

- An option on interest rates, borrowers' options, lenders' options, caps and floors, typically is hedged by buying or selling FRAs.

For example, if a bank writes a borrower's option, its options position gives it an exposure to the risk of a rise in interest rates. The bank can hedge this position by purchasing FRAs. The *quantity* of FRAs to purchase, i.e. the notional principal amount of the FRA, would depend on the option's delta. If the option were written with an at-the-money strike price, its delta would be 0.5, and a delta hedge would be created by purchasing an FRA for a notional principal amount equal to 0.5 times the notional principal amount covered by the option.

The effect of the delta hedge is that if the price of the underlying item (LIBOR) changes, the loss or gain on the option-writer's option's position will be offset by a matching gain or loss on the FRA position.

When the market price of the underlying item changes, the delta of the option also will change, and an adjustment must be made to the delta hedge by purchasing or selling more FRAs.

Example

A bank sells 50 call options on eurodollar futures, and the delta of the options is 0.40. To create a delta hedge, the bank would buy 20 (50 x 0.40) eurodollar futures. Any rise or fall in the value of the options to the writer will be offset by a matching fall or rise in the value of the futures. As the market price of the futures contract changes, the delta of the option also will change. If the delta went up to 0.44, for example, the bank would have to adjust its delta hedge to (50 x 0.44) 22 futures contracts. It would purchase two more futures.

Summary

Options provide a form of conditional hedge. They provide protection against adverse movements in interest rates by fixing a maximum cost on floating-rate borrowing or a minimum yield on floating-rate lending or investing, but are not exercised if market interest rates are more beneficial. They can be used to hedge exposures over the short-to-medium term. Their major drawback is their cost when compared with an FRA or a swap that also can be used to fix an interest rate, but in an unconditional binding agreement.

Interest-Rate Swaps

An interest-rate swap is a contract between two parties, a swaps bank and a customer. The parties agree to exchange (swap) a stream of payments at one interest rate for a stream of payments at a different rate, normally at regular intervals for a period of several years. The interest rates are applied to an agreed notional amount of principal.

The purpose of a swap is to enable the customer to exchange an existing fixed or floating interest-rate commitment for an interest-rate commitment in a different form, but without affecting any underlying loan or investment.

There are two broad types of interest-rate swap: a coupon swap and a basis swap.

- In a coupon swap, one party makes payments at a fixed rate of interest in exchange for receiving payments at a floating rate, that is reset for each payment. The other party pays the floating rate and receives the fixed rate.
- In a basis swap, the parties exchange payments on one floating-rate basis, for example at three-month LIBOR or at a six-month CD rate, for payments on another floating-rate basis, for example at six-month LIBOR or Treasury bill rate.

Most interest-rate swaps are coupon swaps. Also there are cross-currency coupon swaps in which the parties exchange interest payments in one currency for interest in a second currency, on equivalent notional principal amounts in each currency.

Features of Swaps

The exchanges of payments under a swap agreement are based on a notional amount of principal that will be at least $10 million or so, or its equivalent amount in another currency. A swaps bank usually will agree to the amount of notional principal that the customer asks for, subject to an acceptable minimum. Swaps are available in any freely convertible currency, although some banks could be more willing than other to negotiate swaps in particular currencies. For example, an Australian bank will be more willing than a Canadian bank to arrange an interest-rate swap in Australian dollars.

The term of a swap typically is between two and ten years. The term can be as short as one month, but short-term swaps have much in common with FRAs. Swap terms also can be as long as 30 years. The timing of payments between the swap counterparties can be tailored to the requirements of the customer, but it is usual for payments to occur at regular intervals, typically every six months or one year.

The amount payable by each party to the other usually is decided at the start of a notional interest-rate period, but paid at the end of the period. For example, if Alpha and Beta Bank arrange a swap with a six-monthly exchange of payments, the amount payable by each to the other would be calculated at the start of each six-month period, and paid at the end of six months, but only a net payment might be made when both payments are in the same currency. For example, if Alpha must pay Beta Bank $A and Beta Bank must pay $B in return, there will be a net payment of $(A-B) from Alpha to Beta or of $(B-A) from Beta to Alpha, depending on which party must pay the larger amount.

Although it is convenient to refer to them as such, swap payments technically are not interest payments because there is no actual loan between the parties to the swap. Swap payments are payments calculated by applying an interest rate to a notional amount of principal.

Coupon Swaps

In a coupon swap, the parties agree to exchange a stream of payments at a fixed rate of interest for a stream of payments at a floating rate of interest. One party pays the fixed rate and receives the floating-rate payment. The other party receives the fixed rate and makes the floating-rate payment.. The floating rate of interest is a reference market rate, such as three-month LIBOR or six-month LIBOR that is specified in the swap agreement.

Coupon Swap

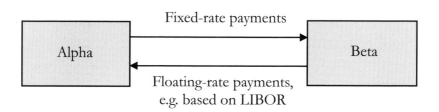

A bank that specializes in swaps transactions will quote a fixed rate that it is prepared to receive and a fixed rate that it is prepared to pay in exchange for floating-rate interest at a reference market rate such as six-month LIBOR. Its quoted receive rate will be higher than its pay rate, and the difference between the two rates represents the profit margin that the bank would expect to make in a two-legged swap transaction.

Swaps Bank as Market Maker

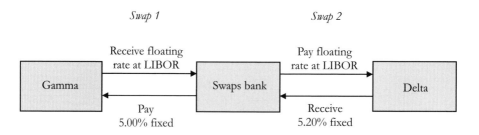

In the diagram opposite, if the swaps bank can arrange matching but opposite swaps with two customers, Gamma and Delta, for the same notional principal amount, it will make a net profit of 20 basis points. This is 0.20% per annum of the notional principal that is the difference between the fixed rate of 5.20% receivable and the 5.0% fixed rate payable on the combined legs of the arrangements with its two customers.

Hedging with Coupon Swaps

Coupon swaps can be used to hedge a long-term exposure to the risk of rising or falling interest rates by allowing the user to manage the mix of fixed-rate and floating-rate obligations in its debt portfolio, or the mix of fixed-rate and floating-rate income in its investment portfolio. Swaps that change payments from fixed rate to floating rate or vice versa for an underlying debt are called liability swaps. Those that change an income stream on investments from fixed to floating rate or vice versa are called asset swaps. Both liability swaps and asset swaps operate in the same way.

- If a company believes that it has an exposure to an increase in interest rates because too much of its borrowing is at floating rate, it can arrange a swap to change some or all of its floating-rate interest obligations into fixed-rate obligations without altering its underlying loans.
- Similarly, if a company believes that it has an exposure to falling interest rates, and that it has too much fixed-rate borrowing at a high fixed rate, it can arrange a swap to change some or all of its fixed-rate interest-rate obligations into variable-rate obligations.

There is an active swaps market and companies should be able to switch from fixed to variable-rate obligations or vice versa without difficulty so as to achieve a suitable floating-rate/fixed-rate mix. The mix can be adjusted whenever required by means of further swap arrangements, without having to redeem actual loans or obtain new loans because swaps do not affect existing loans or investments in any way.

Companies might be unable to borrow long term at a fixed rate directly from a bank or the bond market, but can obtain a loan at a floating rate. If they want to pay interest at a fixed rate, they can borrow at a variable rate and arrange a swap to exchange the floating-rate obligation for a fixed rate.

Example 1

Gamma wants to borrow $30 million for five years, with interest payable at six-monthly intervals. It can borrow this money from a bank at a floating rate for dollar LIBOR plus 100 basis points, but wants to obtain a fixed rate for the full five-year period. A swaps bank indicates that it will be willing to receive a fixed rate of 5.8% in exchange for payments of six-month LIBOR.

Five-Year Swap: Notional Principal $30 million

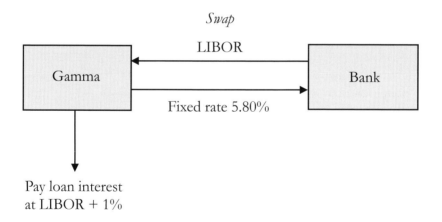

Analysis

Gamma borrows $30 million with interest at six-month LIBOR plus 100 basis points. In the swap, it receives six-month LIBOR and pays fixed interest at 5.80%. The net effect is to acquire a fixed-rate obligation at 6.80% for the full term of the swap.

		%
Borrow at LIBOR plus 100 bp:	Pay	- (LIBOR + 1.0)
Swap	Receive	+ LIBOR
	Pay	- 5.80
Effective borrowing cost		- 6.80

Gamma will fix its payments at about $1,020,000 ($30 million x 6.8% x 6/12) every six months for the five-year term of the swap. Note: The actual payments of interest will be slightly different because of the interest-rate conventions used.

At each six-monthly fixing date for the swap, the payment due from Gamma to the swaps bank or from the bank to Gamma will depend on the market rate for six-month LIBOR at that date.

Outcome 1
Suppose that on the first fixing date for the swap, at the end of month 6 in the first year, six-month LIBOR is 7%. The payments due by each party to the swap will be as follows:

	$
Gamma pays fixed rate of 5.8%	
($30 million x 5.8% x 6/12)	870,000
Swaps bank pays LIBOR rate of 7%	
($30 million x 7% x 6/12)	1,050,000
Net payment from bank to Gamma	180,000

This payment will be made six months later, at the end of the notional interest-rate period. Gamma will pay interest on its loan at LIBOR + 100 basis points, which for this six-month period is 8% (7% + 1%). Taken with the payment received under the swap agreement, the net cost to Gamma is equivalent to interest payable at 6.80%.

	$
Loan payment at 8% ($30 million x 8% x 6/12)	1,200,000
Payment received from the swaps bank	- 180,000
Net effective borrowing cost	1,020,000

Outcome 2

Suppose that at the next six-monthly fixing date, six-month LIBOR is 4.6%. The swap payments will be as follows:

	$
Gamma pays fixed rate of 5.8%	870,000
Swaps bank pays LIBOR rate of 4.6%	
($30 million x 4.6% x 6/12)	690,000
Net payment from Gamma to bank	180,000

Under its loan arrangement, Gamma will pay 5.6% (LIBOR + 100 basis points) for the six-month period. Adding the net swap payment gives a total cost for the six-month period of $1,020,000, equivalent to an interest rate of 6.8% for the period.

	$
Loan payment at 5.6% ($30 million x 5.6% x 6/12)	840,000
Payment to the swaps bank	+ 180,000
All-in effective borrowing cost	1,020,000

Active interest-rate management could involve the arrangement of several swaps over time for the same underlying loan. A company with a long-term floating-rate debt, for example, could swap into fixed rate, and subsequently swap back into floating rate and so on, depending on management's view of future changes in interest rates and the most suitable fixed-rate and floating-rate mix for its debts.

Example 2

Delta borrows £40 million by issuing seven-year bonds at a fixed rate of 5%. It believes that interest rates will soon fall, however, and arranges a swap in which it is a payer of floating rate at LIBOR and a receiver of 4.7% fixed. The net effect is that Delta will pay a floating rate on its loan at LIBOR plus 30 basis points.

		%
Bond interest payment:	Pay	- 5.00
Swap:	Receive	+ 4.70
	Pay	- LIBOR
Effective borrowing cost		- (LIBOR + 0.30)

Suppose that Delta is right and interest rates do fall, but that a year or so later, Delta believes that they might now start to rise again. It decides to arrange another swap in which it receives floating rate (LIBOR) and pays a fixed rate. The fixed-rate payment for the swap is 4%, reflecting lower market interest rates at the time.

Following the second swap, Delta will become a fixed-rate payer again, but at a lower interest rate than the amount payable on the bonds.

		%
Borrow at LIBOR plus 100 bp:	Pay	- 5.00
First swap	Receive	+ 4.70
	Pay	- LIBOR
Second swap:	Receive	+ LIBOR
	Pay	- 4.00
Effective borrowing cost		- 4.30

Basis Swaps

In a basis swap, the parties agree to exchange a stream of floating-rate payments on one basis for a stream of floating-rate payments on a different basis. Floating-rate basis might be three-month LIBOR, six-month LIBOR, a Treasury bill rate, certificate of deposit rate, or a commercial paper rate. Basis swaps are much less common than coupon swaps, but can be used by banks as a hedge against basis risk and gap exposures.

Example
West Bank is partly funded by customer deposits for which it pays interest at six-month LIBOR minus 50 basis points. It has used the funds

to lend at three-month LIBOR, but is concerned about its exposure to a shift in the yield curve and that six-month LIBOR could rise relative to three-month LIBOR.

It arranges a basis swap with another bank in which it receives six-month LIBOR minus 20 basis points, and pays three-month LIBOR.

Five-Year Swap: Notional Principal

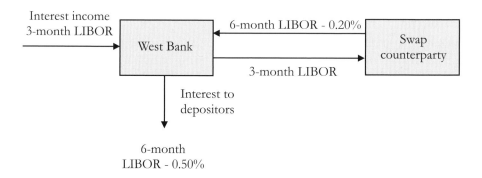

Analysis

By arranging the swap, West Bank matches its income at three-month LIBOR with the amount payable for the swap, and matches the basis for its payments to depositors with the rate receivable from the swap. The net effect is to lock in a profit of 30 basis points on its funding.

		%
Interest paid to depositors	Pay	− (6-month LIBOR− 0.50)
Interest receivable on lending	Receive	+ 3-month LIBOR
Swap	Receive	+ 6-month LIBOR − 0.20
	Pay	− 3 month LIBOR
Net receipts		+ 0.30

Reaching Hedging Decisions

To determine whether to use swaps to hedge interest-rate exposures, a company should first identify all those exposures arising from its long-term corporate funding or investment activity, for maturities of two or more years. It should establish whether the exposures are on a fixed or floating-rate basis and the duration of each. For all but the largest companies this should be a straightforward exercise.

Previous hedging activity should not be overlooked, and the precise interest-rate status of each exposure should be checked and confirmed. The company could have in place several interest-rate hedges for an exposure, for example it might already have a swap to change interest-rate payments from a floating rate to a fixed rate.

The company should then decide on the optimal blend of fixed and floating-rate debt, and the required duration of this optimal blend. The most common split of fixed and floating-rate debt is 50:50, simply because a change in interest rates will have both beneficial and adverse effects that ought to be largely self-canceling.

The required duration of the hedge will depend upon the term of both existing debt and new debt, and also on management's view of whether a hedge is required for the full term of each loan. The most common duration for fixing the cost of debt tends to be five years because this is a standard term for floating-rate bank-loan facilities.

As a result of their analysis, management should establish the company's interest-rate swap requirements in terms of specific amounts and duration, and the terms of each swap, fixed into floating or vice versa, etc. The necessary swaps should then be executed if suitable prices are available.

Advantages of Swaps

Swaps are flexible instruments for managing interest rates for longer-term funding and investments, as a separate measure from managing the debt or investment portfolio. As a hedging instrument, swaps give management any opportunity to:

- manage the fixed/floating-rate balance of debts or investments
- take action in anticipation of future interest-rate changes without having to repay existing loans, take out new loans or alter an investment portfolio.

Fixing the cost of debt for an extended period can improve the credit perception of a company particularly in an environment of rising interest rates, as it reduces a company's financial risk exposures.

There is an active swaps market and positions can be changed over time as required. It is also relatively easy, if necessary, to close a swaps position by termination, reversal or buyout.

Accounting Aspects of Interest-Rate Risk Management

A non-bank company has to be aware of the implications for its balance sheet and profit and loss account of its transactions in financial instruments, including derivatives. Companies might use derivatives to hedge an exposure, or might take speculative positions in derivatives. Some companies, not only banks, might trade in financial instruments to make a profit.

Regulations about how financial instruments should be accounted for and presented in the report and financial accounts of a company are still evolving, but there is now a well-established view that companies should present information about the financial instruments they use and their approach to risk management.

Accounting regulations differ between countries, but this chapter considers some of the issues involved.

Accounting for Financial Instruments

The accounting treatment of financial instruments will differ to some extent between banks and non-bank companies.

- Banks, particularly commercial banks, have very large amounts of financial assets and liabilities in their balance sheet, notably loans and deposits.
- Although non-bank companies might trade in financial instruments, running a trading book is often a major aspect of the operations of a bank, providing an important source of income and profit.

● Many non-bank companies use financial instruments, particularly forward contracts and derivatives, exclusively in order to hedge their exposures to risk. For non-bank companies, the use of derivative instruments arises as a by product out of their main operations.

In the UK, non-bank public companies are required by Financial Reporting Standard FRS13 to provide some information about risk management in their annual report and accounts, including information about the use of derivatives. The information required consist of both narrative and numerical disclosures.

● Narrative disclosures should explain the financial instruments that have been used by the company to create or change its risk profile. The company should explain its objectives and policies in using financial instruments.
● The numerical disclosures are intended to show how the objectives are being achieved and the policies implemented.

Accounting for Financial Futures

When a company buys or sells financial futures as a short-term hedge for an interest-rate exposure, the transactions may be accounted for as follows.

Event	Accounting entries	
	Debit	**Credit**
Pay an initial margin (performance bond) on buying or selling futures	Margin account	Cash
Futures position shows a profit, when marked to market	Margin account	Deferred profit/ loss
Futures position shows a profit, when marked to market	Deferred profit/ loss	Margin account

Event (cont.)	Accounting entries	
	Debt	Credit
Futures exchange calls for additional margin payment, to cover losses on the position	Cash	Margin account
Futures position closed. Balance on margin account repaid to the company	Cash	Margin account
Hedge ended. Profit or loss realized. Report a loss on the hedge	Profit and loss account (loss realized)	Deferred profit/ loss
Or report a profit on the hedge	Deferred profit/ loss	Profit and loss account (profit realized)

Accounting for FRAs

No premium is payable when an FRA is bought or sold. A compensatory payment is made or received when the FRA is settled, at the beginning of the notional interest period to which the FRA relates.

Where an FRA is used as a hedge, the accounting entries are as follows.

Event	Accounting entries	
	Debt	Credit
On settlement date, for gains	Cash	Profit/loss on FRAs account
On settlement date, for losses	Profit/loss on FRAs account	Cash

Accounting for Interest-Rate Swaps

For a plain vanilla swap, used to hedge an interest-rate exposure, there will be a payment, every six months or year, from one swap party to the other. These payments should be matched to the six-month or one-year term of the interest period to which each payment relates, applying the accruals concept of accounting.

Example

On March 31 Year 1, ABC borrows $20 million at a floating rate of six-month LIBOR plus 100 basis points. It also arranges a swap with its bank, receiving six-month LIBOR and paying 6.5% fixed. Swap payments will be every six months, payable at the end of each six-month period.

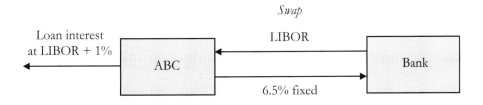

Swap

ABC has obtained fixed-rate funds at 7.5% net.

		%
Interest on loan	Pay	– (LIBOR + 1.0)
Swap:	Receive	LIBOR
	Pay	– 6.5
Net interest cost		– 7.5

Suppose that the company's accounting year-end is December 31 and that six-month LIBOR is:

- 6% at March 31 of that year, and

● 5% at September 30 of that year.

In the profit and loss account of ABC for year to December 31, the borrowing costs and swap payments will be recorded as follows:

	$
Borrowing costs on $20 million	
Six months to September 30 (at 7%)	700,000
Three months to December 31, accrued (at 6%)	300,000
	1,000,000
Swap payments	
Six months to September 30, paid (0.50%)	50,000
Three months to December 31, accrued (1.5%)	75,000
Total interest cost	1,125,000

These interest costs should be shown in the profit and loss account of the company for the year to 31 December, totalling nine months' interest on $20 million at 7.5%.

In its balance sheet as at 31 December, the company will include a creditor for the swap payment payable, relating to the three-month period September 30-December 31, of $75,000. The balance sheet as at December 31 will include:

	$
Creditor for accrued interest on loan for three months from September 30, payable on March 31	300,000
Swap payment owed relating to three months from September 30, payable on March 31	75,000
	375,000

The balance sheet also will include the actual loan of $20 million, but not the notional amount of principal on which the swap is based. The company will include the variable-rate loan of $20 million within its fixed-rate funding at an interest cost of 7.5%, because of the swap.

Accounting for Borrowers' and Lenders' Options

The premium for the buyer of an option can be accounted for in one of three ways:

- It can be written off in full against profit at the time the option is purchased.
- It can be written off at the time of expiry/exercise of the option.
- It can be amortized over the life of the option.

Any of the three alternative accounting treatments could be justified. It would be difficult, however, for an option writer to justify the immediate booking of the full premium as sales revenue in the P&L account.

Accounting for Interest-Rate Caps

The cost of the premium should be treated as an asset, and amortized over the period of the cap.

Example
A cap has a term of five years and the premium costs $500,000.

When the cap is purchased the accounting entry for the payment will be as follows:

- Credit: Cash $500,000
- Debit: Cap premium account $500,000

The cap premium is an asset, and would appear in the company's balance sheet. Like other long-term assets, its cost must be depreciated (amortized) over its life. Each year, one fifth of the cap premium can be amortized and written off as a cost to the profit and loss account.

| Credit: | Cap premium account | $100,000 |
| Debit: | Profit and loss account | $100,000 |

Receipts under a cap agreement normally are paid in arrears at the end of the interest-rate period, and at an accounting year-end there may be a debtor for a payment receivable. The accruals concept should be applied, and only the portion of any payment receivable that applies to the current accounting year should be brought into the P & L account.

Accounting entries for caps areas follows:

- At the beginning of the six-month period to which the cap payment relates to

  Debit   Debtor for cap payment receivable

  Credit   Cap payments receivable.

- Receivable cap payments to be treated as finance income for the year will be accounted for by a transfer to the profit and loss account

  Debit   Cap payments receivable

  Credit   profit and loss account

- When the cash payment is received, the cash receipt is recorded as

  Debit   Cash

  Credit   Debtor for cap payment receivable

Accounting for floors and collars is done in a similar way.

Appendix: Duration and Immunizing a Bond Portfolio

Fund managers, responsible for the management of investment funds or pension funds, might use a form of structural hedging for their bond portfolios, based on the concepts of

- the duration of the bonds in the portfolio, and
- immunizing a portfolio.

These concepts are explained in this appendix.

Duration

The duration of a bond can be used to measure the price volatility of a bond in response to a change in market interest rates.

To understand duration, it will be useful to begin by looking first of all at the concept of futurity, and the term to the maturity of a bond.

Futurity
The futurity of a bond is a measurement of how long on average an investor must wait to receive the interest and the principal repayment on redemption from a bond. A bond with ten years to maturity, for example, will have a longer futurity than a bond with just two years to maturity. However, the futurity of a ten-year bond normally will be less than ten years because some income is received by the bond investor in the period up to maturity, in the form of interest payments.

Futurity can differ between bonds with the same remaining term to maturity because of their different coupon rates of interest.

Example

Three different bonds each have exactly four years remaining to redemption, but they have different coupon rates of interest. Interest is paid annually in each case. The expected returns to bondholders up to maturity and redemption are, per $100 of bonds:

Bond	Coupon	Year 1	Year 2	Year 3	Year 4	Total returns
		$	$	$	$	$
Bond A	Zero	0	0	0	100	100
Bond B	5%	5	5	5	105	120
Bond C	10%	10	10	10	110	140

Bond A is a zero coupon bond, and bondholders will receive nothing until redemption when they will receive a payment equal to the face value of the bond. Bonds B and C have coupons of 5% and 10% respectively.

Analysis

Although the three bonds have the same remaining term of four years to maturity, the cash returns to investors have a different profile or spread in each case. For Bond A, the investor must wait four years for any return. For Bond B, interest at 5% is receivable in years 1, 2 and 3, representing 15/120 of the total investment returns to maturity. For Bond C, interest at 10% is receivable in years 1, 2 and 3, representing 30/140 of the total investment returns to maturity.

The average time that the investor has to wait for the returns is greatest for Bond A and least for Bond C. The average waiting time can be measured as the futurity of the bond.

Measuring Futurity

One method of measuring futurity is to calculate, for each bond, a weighted average of the time periods, i.e. a weighted average number of years the bond investor must wait for the cash returns. Year 1 returns are given a weighting of 1, year 2 returns a weighting of 2, year 3 returns a weighting of 3, and so on.

The weighted average calculation can be shown by the following formula:

$$\text{Futurity} = \frac{(R_1 \times 1) + (R_2 \times 2) + (R_3 \times 3) + \ldots + (R_n \times n)}{R_1 + R_2 + R_3 + \ldots + R_4}$$

In our example, the futurity of the three bonds is as follows.

Bond A $\quad \dfrac{0(1) + 0(2) + 0(3) + 100(4)}{(0 + 0 + 0 + 100)} \quad = \quad \dfrac{400}{100} \quad = \quad 4.0 \text{ years}$

Bond B $\quad \dfrac{5(1) + 5(2) + 5(3) + 105(4)}{(5 + 5 + 5 + 105)} \quad = \quad \dfrac{450}{120} \quad = \quad 3.75 \text{ years}$

Bond C $\quad \dfrac{10(1) + 10(2) + 10(3) + 110(4)}{(10 + 10 + 10 + 110)} \quad = \quad \dfrac{500}{140} \quad = \quad 3.57 \text{ years}$

These measurements show that the average waiting period for returns is a full four years for Bond A, less for Bond B and least for Bond C that has the highest coupon.

Macaulay's Duration

A weakness of this measurement of futurity is that the weightings give equal value to returns in each of the years to maturity of the bonds. For example, $1 receivable in Year 4 is given equal value as $1 receivable in Year 1. Because money has a time value, and income can be reinvested, cash receipts in earlier years have greater value to an investor than cash flows in later years. The time value of money can be allowed for by discounting the future cash flows from each bond to a present value.

The discounted value of a future cash flow is:

$$\frac{R_n}{(1 + i)^n}$$

Where:

- R is the cash return in Year n
- i is the rate of discount that is the current redemption yield on the bond. $7\% = 0.07$, etc.

A measure of futurity incorporating present values is known as Macaulay's duration. The formula is as follows.

$$D = \frac{\dfrac{(R_1 \times 1)}{(1+i)^1} + \dfrac{(R_2 \times 2)}{(1+i)^2} + \dfrac{(R_3 \times 3)}{(1+i)^3} + \ldots + \dfrac{(R_n \times n)}{(1+i)^n}}{\dfrac{R_1}{(1+i)^1} + \dfrac{R_2}{(1+i)^2} + \dfrac{R_3}{(1+i)^3} + \ldots + \dfrac{R_n}{(1+i)^n}}$$

Note that the weightings below the line in the formula must be at discounted values, just like the cash flow values above the line.

This formula can be simplified a little, to:

$$D = \frac{(PV_1 \times 1) + (PV_2 \times 2) + (PV_3 \times 3) + \ldots + (PV_n \times n)}{MV}$$

Where:

- MV is the market value of the bond
- PV_1, PV_2, PV_3 ... PV_n represent the present value of the cash flow each year from the bond, up to maturity in Year n.

The cash flows are discounted at the bond's redemption yield.

Example
Returning to the previous example, suppose the current redemption yield on all three bonds is 8% per annum. The market value of each bond, and the present value of each year's cash flow for each bond, is as follows:

Year	Discount factor at 8%	Bond A		Bond B		Bond C	
		Cash $	PV $	Cash $	PV $	Cash $	PV $
1	$\dfrac{1}{(1.08)^1}$	0	0.00	5	4.63	10	9.26
2	$\dfrac{1}{(1.08)^2}$	0	0.00	5	4.29	10	8.57
3	$\dfrac{1}{(1.08)^3}$	0	0.00	5	3.97	10	7.94
4	$\dfrac{1}{(1.08)^4}$	100	73.50	105	77.18	110	80.85
			73.50		90.07		106.62

The duration (Macaulay's duration) for each bond is calculated as follows.

$$\text{Bond A} \quad \frac{0(1) + 0(2) + 0(3) + 73.50(4)}{73.50} \quad = \quad 4.0 \text{ years}$$

$$\text{Bond B} \quad \frac{4.63(1) + 4.29(2) + 3.97(3) + 77.18(4)}{90.07} \quad = \quad 3.7 \text{ years}$$

$$\text{Bond C} \quad \frac{9.26(1) + 8.57(2) + 7.94(3) + 80.85(4)}{106.62} \quad = \quad 3.5 \text{ years}$$

Once again, the duration is longest for the zero coupon bond, Bond A, and is shortest for Bond C that has the highest coupon. The duration of every zero coupon bond is always exactly its full remaining term to maturity.

This example of duration uses bonds with an annual interest payment. Duration also can be calculated for bonds where interest is paid semi-annually. The discount rate, i.e. the redemption yield, is simply converted from an annual rate to a six-monthly rate, and the same formula for calculating duration is then applied to the six-monthly cash flows on the bond.

Factors that Determine Duration
In the previous example, all the bonds had the same maturity, four years, and only their coupons differed. Remember, however, that duration also will differ according to the remaining term to maturity of the bond. Short-dated bonds will have a shorter duration than longer-dated bonds.

The three factors that determine the duration of a bond are:

- the remaining term to redemption
- the coupon rate for the bond
- the current redemption yield on the bond, that is used as the discount rate in the calculation of duration.

Duration and Bond Price Volatility
The relevance of duration to bond investors and dealers is that the price volatility of a bond, in response to a change in the current market interest rate (yield) for bonds, varies directly according to its duration. Duration is a measure of the price sensitivity of a bond in response to a change in interest rates. The mathematical proof of this relationship is beyond the scope of this book, but the formula showing the relationship is:

$$\frac{\Delta P}{\Delta i} = -D \left[\frac{P}{\left(1 + \frac{i}{2}\right)} \right]$$

Where:

- Δ means a change in
- P is the price of the bond
- i is the market rate of interest on the bond (current bond yield)
- D is the duration of the bond (Macaulay's duration)

Modified Duration
For simplicity, investors use a modified measurement of duration rather than duration itself. Modified duration D_m is

$$D_m = \frac{D}{\left(1 + \frac{i}{2}\right)}$$

Example

A bond has a duration, measured by Macaulay's duration, of 3.5 years. The current redemption yield on the bond is 8%. Its modified duration therefore is $3.5/(1.04) = 3.36$ years.

Since:

$$\frac{\Delta P}{\Delta i} = -D\left[\frac{P}{\left(1 + \dfrac{i}{2}\right)}\right]$$

it follows that:

$$\frac{\Delta P}{\Delta i} = -D_m P$$

Re-arranging this, we get:

$$\frac{\Delta P}{P} = -D_m \Delta i$$

$\Delta P/P$ is simply a proportional change in the price of the bond. This formula can be used to calculate the proportional change in the price of a bond that could be expected from a change in the market rate of interest (Δi), provided the duration of the bond is known.

An important assumption, however, is that the duration, and modified duration, of a bond is the same at all price levels of the bond. In practise, it has been found that the modified duration of a bond is roughly constant over a fairly wide range of interest rates (yields and prices). This assumption of a constant value for duration therefore is reasonably accurate and reliable.

Example

A bond has a current market value of 106.62. Its current redemption yield is 8%, and its modified duration is 3.36 years.

Analysis

If interest rates were to go up by 10 basis points, so that the bond investor requires a yield of 8.10% on the bond, the price of the bond would fall. The fall in price from an increase of 10 basis points in the yield (0.0010) would be:

$$\frac{\Delta P}{P} = -D_m \Delta i = -3.36\,(0.0010) = = -0.0036 = -0.336\%$$

The price would fall by 0.336%, to 99.664% of its previous value. In other words, the bond price will fall from 106.62 to 106.26, a fall of 0.36.

Using Duration

Investment managers who are responsible for a portfolio of fixed-rate bonds can use measurements of duration to control the price-risk/ interest-rate risk in their investment portfolio. A manager can establish the approximate effect on the total value of the portfolio from a given change in interest rates. Bonds with a high duration could be avoided, particularly when market interest rates are more likely to rise than to fall in the future.

Immunizing a Portfolio

The concept of duration also can be used by fund managers to immunize their fixed income bond portfolio against the effects of a change in interest rates.

Suppose for example that a pension fund has a liability of $100 million that it must pay in five years' time. If there were no interest-rate risk, the fund manager could decide to buy some bonds maturing in five years' time, and use the income from the bonds to meet the liability.

The quantity of bonds the fund manager would buy would have to provide sufficient interest, reinvested at the same yield as obtainable on the bonds for example, so that together with the redemption of the bonds at maturity, there would be sufficient money to meet the liability in full.

Interest-rate risk complicates the fund manager's decision. If he/she buys a quantity of bonds and interest rates change:

- the market value of the bonds will change, and
- the yield obtainable from reinvesting the interest received from the bonds also will change.

A change in interest rates could mean that the total fund available to meet the future liability might be insufficient to cover the liability in full.

The risk can be avoided to a large degree by purchasing bonds with the same duration as the liability. For a liability of $100 million in five years' time, a fund manager can buy bonds that have the same duration five years. The amount of bonds purchased would have to be sufficient to produce interest (reinvested) plus capital totalling $100 million after five years. One way of doing this would be to purchase a quantity of zero coupon bonds maturing in five years' time that will pay out $100 million on redemption. This is one reason why zero coupon bonds and bond strips are popular with fund managers.

Immunization also would be achieved by purchasing a longer-dated bond but with a duration of five years.

Example
A fund has to meet a liability of $10 million in 3.5 years' time. It purchases a bond with a duration of 3.5 years to immunize itself against the risk of changing bond interest rates (yields). The details of the bond purchased are:

Coupon	10%
Interest payable	annually, the next in 12 months' time
Term to redemption	4 years
Current redemption yield	8%
Current market value	106.62

Note
This is Bond C, whose duration was calculated earlier in this Appendix.

Analysis
Each $100 (nominal value) of the bonds should yield the following cash after 3.5 years, on the assumptions that:

- after 3.5 years, the bond will be sold in the market at a price based on a redemption yield of 8%, and
- interest received until then will be reinvested to earn interest at 8% per annum.

Item	Amount	Value after 3.5 years
	$	$
Year 1 interest	$10 \times (1.08)^{2.5}$	12.12
Year 2 interest	$10 \times (1.08)^{1.5}$	11.22
Year 3 interest	$10 \times (1.08)^{0.5}$	10.39
Sale of bond. Year 3.5	$110 \times (1.08)^{-0.5}$	105.85
		139.58

To meet a liability of $10 million after 3.5 years, the fund manager would buy $7,164,350 (nominal value) of the bonds, $10 million ÷ 139.58/100.

Suppose that as soon as the bonds have been purchased, the market yield on the bonds rises from 8% to 9%. The market price of the bonds will fall, but interest received from the bonds can be reinvested at 9%. Each $100 (nominal value) of the bonds will now yield the following sum after 3.5 years.

Item	Amount	Value after 3.5 years
	$	$
Year 1 interest	$10 \times (1.09)^{2.5}$	12.40
Year 2 interest	$10 \times (1.09)^{1.5}$	11.38
Year 3 interest	$10 \times (1.09)^{0.5}$	10.44
Sale of bond. Year 3.5	$110 \times (1.09)^{-0.5}$	105.36
		139.58

The same quantity of bonds will be sufficient to meet the liability of $10 million in 3.5 years' time. The fall in the sale value of the bond at the end of 3.5 years is offset by the improved reinvestment income from the interest received. This happens because the fund's asset, the bonds, have the same duration as the liability.

Glossary

Basis Point
One hundredth of 1% (0.01%.)

Basis Risk
The risk that interest rates on one type of financial instrument, e.g. Treasury bills, will become less favorable in comparison to interest rates on another type of financial instrument, e.g. interbank lending at LIBOR. Basis risk exists when there is a mismatch between a hedge and an underlying instrument caused by a difference in the interest basis for each.

Basis Swap
A swap from one floating rate to another, e.g. three-month LIBOR rate in exchange for six-month LIBOR rate.

Benchmark Rate
A rate of interest in the financial markets against which other interest rates are set, or against which transactions in some financial instruments are settled.

Bond Future
Future contract for which the underlying item purchased or sold is a standard quantity of notional government bonds

Borrower's Option
An option that gives its holder the right but not the obligation on or before an expiry date to borrow a specified quantity of notional funds for a specified term and at a specified rate of interest, from some future date.

Cap

An interest-rate cap is a series of borrowers' options that sets a maximum interest rate on medium-term, variable-rate borrowing. An option will be exercised at each rollover date for the loan, over the term of the cap agreement, if the current market rate of interest exceeds the strike price in the cap.

Caption

An option to buy a cap.

Collar

A combination of a cap and a floor. The collar holder buys a cap and sells a floor, or buys a floor and sells a cap, to fix a maximum and minimum interest rate on borrowing or lending. The advantage of a collar over a cap or floor is a lower premium.

Coupon Rate

Rate of interest payable on the nominal value of issued bonds or loan stock.

Coupon Swap

An interest-rate swap in which the parties swap fixed for floating-rate payments. Also called a fixed/floating swap.

Cross-Currency Coupon Swap

A currency swap combined with an interest-rate coupon swap, a swap of fixed-rate payments in one currency for floating-rate payments in another currency.

Currency Swap

A transaction in which two parties, a bank and a another company, agree to swap fixed or floating-rate cash flows in equivalent amounts of two different currencies for a specific period.

Derivative

A financial security, such as an option, swap or future, whose value is derived in part from the value and characteristics of another underlying security or instrument. In the case of interest-rate options, the underlying instrument is a notional loan or deposit.

Eurobond
Marketable bond (debt security) issued outside the country in whose currency the debt is denominated.

Exposure
A financial risk facing a business. An exposure can be categorized according to its cause or source.

Financial Risk
The risk of profits being affected by unexpected changes in financial conditions or circumstances.

Fixed Rate
An interest rate that does not vary during the life of a transaction.

Forward/Forward Rate
A rate of interest for a future interest period that can be derived from spot interest rates. For example a six-month interest rate for an interest period starting in two months' time can be derived from spot interest rates for two months and eight months.

Forward/Forward Transaction
An arrangement, not much used since the development of FRAs, to fix the cost of future short-term borrowing. The principal is borrowed now at a fixed rate to the end of the planned term and simultaneously invested at a fixed rate until the start of the borrowing term.

Floating Rate
An interest rate that is reset at predetermined intervals, reset dates or rollover dates, during the life of a transaction, e.g. a loan. Also called variable rate.

Floor
A series of lenders' options that sets a minimum interest-rate income for

medium-term variable-rate lending or investments. An option will be exercised at each interest-rate reset date during the term of the floor agreement, if the current market rate of interest is below the strike price of the floor.

Future

An interest-rate future is an exchange-traded contract for the purchase and sale of a standard quantity of a money-market instrument, e.g. a three-month deposit, or government bonds, at an agreed interest rate or price, and for delivery at a specified future date.

Gap Exposure

The risk to profits from adverse movements in interest rates in the time between setting or resetting interest rates on borrowed funds and setting or resetting interest rates on invested funds.

Gearing Ratio

Ratio of debt capital to equity. Measure of the debt burden of companies, and so a basic measure of financial risk.

Generic Swap

Interest-rate swap that has a zero value to each party when first transacted.

Hedge Accounting

Accounting for a financial instrument that is used as a hedge for an exposure. The gain or loss on the hedge transaction is not realized in the profit and loss account of the company until the loss or gain is realized on the underlying transaction or instrument for which it provides a hedge.

Interest Cover

The ratio of profit before interest and tax (PBIT) to interest charges over the same period. (Cover = PBIT ÷ interest charges.)

Lender's Option

A put option that gives its holder the right but not the obligation to deposit a specified quantity of notional principal for a specified term and at a specified rate of interest, from a period starting on or before a specified future date.

LIBID

London Interbank Bid Rate. Theoretically the rate in the interbank money market at which a prime bank will deposit funds with another prime bank. LIBID typically is 12.5 basis points below LIBOR.

LIBOR

London Interbank Offered Rate. Theoretically the rate in the interbank money market at which a prime bank will lend short-term to another prime bank. LIBOR is commonly used as the index or benchmark rate for settlement of financial transactions such as swaps, FRAs, options, etc. Variable-rate lending to many companies is priced at a margin above LIBOR.

Long

See Position.

Netting

Arrangement between bank accounts whereby surpluses in some accounts are transferred to accounts in deficit.

Open Position

See Position.

Plain Vanilla Coupon Swap

A coupon swap that is traded for standard periods of two, three, five, seven, ten years, etc., where payments by each party are based on the same notional principal and which has a zero value when first transacted.

Position

Term to describe the trading position of a buyer or seller of futures. An open position is either long or short. A long position occurs when a trader/company has purchased futures without selling a matching quantity. A short position occurs when a trader/company has sold futures without buying a matching quantity. A position is closed before delivery date when the holder of a long position sells a matching quantity of futures or the holder of a short position buys a matching quantity.

Reset Date/Rollover Date

A date on which the rate of interest on a variable-rate transaction, for example a loan is adjusted, usually to a current market rate. The new rate is then applied to the transaction until the next reset date.

Short

See Position.

STIR

Short-term interest-rate future. Future contract for which the underlying item is a notional short-term (usually three-month) deposit of funds.

Structural Hedging

The reduction or elimination of exposures by matching assets and liabilities in the balance sheet, or income and expenditure. For hedging interest-rate risk, it involves matching borrowing and lending on the same interest-rate basis and for the same borrowing/investment term.

Swap

An agreement between two parties to exchange a series of future payments. In an interest-rate swap, the exchange of payments is from one interest rate to another.

Swaption

Option to enter into a swap agreement.

Variable Rate

See Floating Rate.

Withholding Tax

Tax arrangement whereby interest or dividend payments are made net of tax to a recipient, and withheld by the payer of the interest or dividends for payment to the tax authorities. The recipient might be able to reclaim the tax deducted by the tax authorities.

Yield Curve

A term used to describe how current interest rates vary according to the term-to-maturity of the loan or deposit. When long-term interest rates are higher than shorter-term rates, the yield curve is upward sloping or normal. When long-term interest rates are lower than short-term rates, the yield curve is inverse. These interest-rate comparisons can be shown on a graph; hence the term yield curve.

Index